The Big Ideas Club Presents
Poetic Philosophy
Narrative Translations Designed for Accessibility

Cicero's De Oratare Book I
Dialogic Reasoning

By Cicero

Translated by Jason Kassel, PhD

A Meta-Letter to Brother Quintus (55 BCE)

I.   Mourning the Loss of Leisure-with-Dignity

Quintus, my Brother -

As I often reflect - calling back to Memory the things of old - it always seems to me that, inside the Best Kind of Republic, those Aristocratic-Men were truly blessed who, having been freed from the burdens of animal laborens, were able to dwell fully within the Res Publica. There, they flourished in honors, in the glory of accomplished deeds, and yet still shaped their lives in such a way that they could either engage in political activity without danger or remain inside Leisure-with-Dignity (otium cum dignitate).

There was, in fact, a time when I too believed that it would be just - and almost universally permitted - for me to enter into otium and turn the power of the Mind back to the Noble Studies which belong to us both. I imagined that once the endless toil inside the Forum and the restless striving of ambition had ceased - once the cycle of civic offices had been completed, and the arc of age begun to bend - I would be allowed to return to thought. But that hope - shaped by reflection and guided by intention - was broken, both by the heavy weight of our shared age and by the varied misfortunes that befell me personally. For the very place that had seemed it would be most full of quiet and tranquility - otium itself -

became instead the site of the heaviest burdens and the most turbulent civic storms.Nor was I granted the long - desired fruit of Leisure-with-Dignity: to practice and reflect upon the Arts to which we had been devoted since boyhood. We were not permitted to return to them - neither to cultivate them in Public nor to revive them together in private.

From our earliest years, we were thrust into the collapse of the old educational order; then, during the consulship, we were cast into the very center of every contest and Public danger. And in all the time since, we have been flung headlong into those waves - waves that, though we turned them back from the Republic as a whole, now come crashing down upon us personally. Still, whether through the harshness of circumstances or the narrow confines of time, I will yield to our shared passion for learning. And whatever portion of otium I may be granted from the deception of enemies, the causes of friends, or the Republic herself - I will devote it, above all, to writing.

As for you, my brother -

I will not fail you, whether you urge me or entreat me. No one has greater authority with me, and none could possess more of my goodwill.

II.   A Memory: Eloquence or Systematic-Learning

I must now recall - though not with perfect clarity - a certain Memory from long ago. This recollection, though indistinct in its details, seems to me aptly suited to your request: namely, that you might come to Understand what certain Aristocratic-Men - supremely Eloquent and held in the highest regard - have thought about the full Method and nature of Public-Speech (ratio dicendi). For, as you have often reminded me, those early fragments we produced in youth and adolescence, those passages scrawled in our little notebooks, now seem hardly worthy of the age and Experience we have gained, through so many and such great causes in both Law and the Res Publica. I ought now to set forth something more complete and polished on these very matters.

You are accustomed, too, to differ with me in our conversations on this subject: for I maintain that Eloquence (eloquentia) is bound to the Arts and Education of the wisest Aristocratic-Men - whereas you believe that it ought to be separated from Systematic Learning (doctrina) and entrusted instead to the realm of Natural-Talent and Practical-Habit. But for my part - as I have often looked upon those endowed with the highest capacities - it has always seemed a question worthy of asking: Why is it that more Aristocratic-Men have attained excellence in nearly every other Art than in Public-Speech?

For wherever you direct your Mind and attention, you will find in each discipline many who are not merely adequate, but nearly peerless in their mastery. Indeed, who, judging by the full Knowledge and social and moral authority (auctoritas) of our most distinguished countrymen, would not rank the Commander above the Orator, whether by usefulness or greatness? And yet - who would deny that this single Republic has produced a near-countless multitude of excellent military leaders, while those who have truly excelled in Oratory can scarcely be counted on one's fingers?

Even more striking is this: if we look to history, and to those who have ruled and guided the Republic by counsel and Wisdom, we find many such men in our own time, more still in the generation of our Fathers, and yet more among the Ancients. But truly great Orators - those whose Public-Speech could endure the test of time - have been missing for long stretches; and in nearly every age, barely a single one can be found. And should anyone be tempted to compare the Art of Public-Speech not with the greatness of Command or the clarity of Statesmanship, but with those recondite disciplines immersed in literary subtlety and hidden learning, let him look around at how many Aristocratic-Men have flourished in those very Arts. In this way, he will easily judge just how rare the true Orator has always been - and remains still.

III.   The Rare Orator is Rarest Among the Arts

Surely you are not unaware that there exists a kind of Source and Mother of all the celebrated Arts - what the Greeks name Philosophia - which is held in the highest esteem by the most learned of Aristocratic-Men. Within that Domain, it is difficult even to count how many have attained how much Knowledge, or how wide and abundant a range of disciplines they have brought together under a single Human-Mind. Not confined to a single corner of thought, they sought to gather and synthesize all Knowledge available - whether through Systematic Understanding (scientia) or the practiced Art of Rational Disputation.

And who does not recognize that those whom we call Mathematicians - despite the obscurity of their subject, its hidden difficulty, and subtle complexity - have nonetheless produced a great many accomplished and well-formed Aristocratic-Men? So much so, that hardly anyone who has devoted himself to that Art with serious intensity has failed to acquire what he set out to learn. Likewise, whoever has applied himself to the Art of music, or to that branch of letters cultivated by the grammarians, has usually attained a comprehensive Understanding of the near-limitless force and substance of those disciplines, through reflective study and the deep grasp of Knowledge. Indeed, I would go so far as to say this: that among all the Aristocratic-Men who - once freed from the toils of animal laborens - have received their education in the Liberal Arts and devoted themselves earnestly to these Noble Pursuits, the number of truly great Poets and Orators is exceedingly small. And even within that already rare class - if one were to compare Roman writers with the Greeks - you would still find far fewer accomplished Orators than you would find capable Poets.

IV. The Greek Predicate

Nor can it rightly be said that other Arts have attracted more Aristocratic-Men, or that they entice with greater pleasure, or offer richer hopes, or promise higher rewards to those who study them. Even if we set aside Greece - always striving to be preeminent in Public-Speech - and even pass over Athens itself, the Inventor and Perfecter of all systematic Knowledge, where the full power of Eloquence was both discovered and brought to its final form - even here, in our own Republic, there has never been a time when the pursuit of Eloquence burned with greater intensity. For once our Republic had extended dominion over all peoples, and the Long-Peace secured the possibility of life within Leisure-with-Dignity (otium cum dignitate), nearly every young

Aristocratic-Man - eager for honor - believed he must apply all his effort to attaining mastery in Public-Speech.

At first, of course, they were ignorant of any Method - believing there to be no system of training, no Rules of Art - and they achieved what they could by mere Natural-Capacity (ingenium) and Thoughtful-Reflection. But later, after hearing the Greek Orators, studying their writings, and entering into the discipline of their teachers, our countrymen were seized by an extraordinary zeal for Eloquence. They were stirred not only by ambition, but by the sheer scale and variety of legal and political causes before them - a multitude of every kind - which demanded Theoretical-Preparation, acquired through Private-Study, and frequent Lived-Experience, inside the Forum. And that direct Lived-Experience proved more instructive than any system of rules or any theoretical master. Moreover, the greatest rewards lay plainly in sight, as they still do now: Power, Wealth, and Civic-Honor were all accessible through command of Public-Speech. And, if we judge from repeated examples, the Native-Capacities (ingenia) of our Roman stock have far surpassed those of all other peoples.

Given all this, who would not rightly marvel that, in the whole Memory of all Ages, all Places, and all Republics, so few true Orators are to be found? Surely, then, this Art must be something greater than

Aristocratic-Men typically assume - something compounded from many other Arts, and requiring a rare harmony of elements drawn from the entire range of disciplines.

V. Magnitude of Task

What, then, could explain it - amidst such a vast multitude of Aristocratic-Men as students, with so many teachers, the most gifted of Human-Minds, an infinite variety of causes inside the Forum, and the highest honors promised to Eloquence - what else, I ask, could account for the rarity of truly great Orators, except for the nearly unimaginable magnitude and difficulty of the task itself? For the Orator must possess a wide-ranging grasp of Real-Things - without which a torrent of words becomes empty, absurd, and laughable. His Public-Speech must be shaped not only through precise selection of words, but through the harmony of Structure, Order, and Form. He must thoroughly Understand all the Emotions that nature has implanted in the Human-Condition, for the entire force and logic of Public-Speech lies in its ability to move or restrain the Minds of those who listen.

To all this must be added: charm and wit, a refinement of culture worthy of a Free Man, swiftness in response, sharpness in provocation, all suffused with subtle delight and urbanitas - that grace of the city-born soul. Moreover, the Orator must be steeped in the weight of Memory and the persuasive force of historical example. Nor may he neglect Knowledge of the Laws and the civic framework of the Res Publica. And what should I say of the Act itself - Delivery (actio) - which must be governed by the motion of the body, the gestures of the hand, the expression of the face, and the modulation, rhythm, and variety of the voice? One need only look to the Light-Art of the Stage to grasp the difficulty: there, actors Labor with great intensity to control posture, movement, and sound - and yet, who does not know how few among them earn even passing admiration? What, too, of the sacred treasury of all things - Memory - which must be summoned as the guardian of all that has been discovered and formed in both thought and Speech? For we all Understand that without Memory, even the most excellent Capacities in an Orator vanish into air.

Let us, then, no longer wonder that Eloquence is rare. It arises from the Totality of these elements - each of which, taken alone, demands immense Labor and lifelong Discipline. Instead, let us teach our children - and all whose dignity we cherish - to embrace the vastness of the endeavor. Let them believe that what they seek cannot be gained by the same precepts, the same instructors, or the same shallow exercises as others - but only through rarer, deeper, and higher efforts altogether.

VI. Roman Leisure-with-Dignity and Orator are Superior to Greek Dialectic

In my Judgment, no Aristocratic-Man can be called a True-Orator, crowned with the fullness of praise, unless he has attained Knowledge of all the great matters and of all the Liberal Arts. For Public-Speech must blossom and overflow from the deep wellspring of Real-Things; and if there is no substance beneath the Speech - no thing rightly Grasped and Comprehended by the Orator - then the Language becomes hollow, its Sound almost childish in tone. Yet I do not wish to place so heavy a burden - especially on our Roman Orators, who are encumbered by the urgent business of the City and the burdens of the Res Publica - as to suggest they must know everything and never fall into ignorance.

Still, the very Power and Profession of the Orator - this commitment to Speak-Well in Public - seems to require and promise this: that concerning any matter whatsoever that might be proposed, the Orator will be able to Speak both Fully and Elegantly. And yet, because I do not doubt that this Orator-Ideal may appear to most as something immense, even boundless - especially since even the Greeks, who abound not only in Natural-Capacity and Systematic-Learning, but also in Leisure-with-Dignity and a devotion to study - have divided the Arts into discrete Domains, and no single Aristocratic-

Man has attempted to master them all. They even set aside, from the entire Domain of Speech, that portion concerned with Legal-Disputes and Political-Deliberations, assigning that single portion alone to the Orator.

And so, in these books, I will not seek to encompass more than what has already been assigned - after much inquiry and deliberation - to this kind of Forensic and Civic Oratory by the near-unanimous consensus of the highest-ranking Aristocratic-Men. I will not trace a course of instruction from infancy - I will not begin with the early Grammar of our childish Latin lessons, developed in the shelter of Leisure and free from animal laborens. Instead, I will recall those discussions I once heard among the most Eloquent of our countrymen - Aristocratic-Men who were foremost not only in Speech, but in every Civic Honor and Dignitas. This is not because I scorn the insights handed down by those Greek masters and teachers of Speech. Their writings are available to all, and their paths are open and Public. Nor do I believe that by my interpretation those Greek writings could be made either more Gracious or more Clear.

Therefore - Brother -

If I may ask this small allowance of you, grant me this: that I place, above the teachings of the Greeks, the Authority of those to whom our fellow citizens have awarded the highest praise in the Domain of Public-Speech.

A Gathering in the Year Crassus Dies (91 BCE)

VII. Crassus' Villa (Tusculum): Plato's Phaedrus

At the time when Consul Philippus had begun to escalate his attacks against the Senate's leading Aristocratic-Men, and the Tribunate of Drusus - undertaken in defense of the Senate's Authority - seemed already to be wavering and near collapse, I remember hearing that, during the days of the Roman Games, Lucius Crassus, as if retreating from the Forum to recollect himself, had withdrawn into Leisure-with-Dignity at his Villa in Tusculum.

It was said that Crassus' former father-in-law, Quintus Mucius Scaevola, had gone along as well as Marcus Antonius, who was united with Crassus not only by Public Counsel in the Res Publica, but also by the closest Friendship. Two young Aristocratic-Men had also accompanied Crassus: Gaius Cotta and Publius Sulpicius. Both were especially close to Drusus, and at that time were regarded by their elders as promising heirs to the honors of civic life. Cotta was then a candidate for the Tribunate of the Plebs, and Sulpicius was expected to seek the office in the following year.

On the first day at Crassus' Villa in Tusculum, these Aristocratic-Men - gathered in a moment marked by political urgency - spoke at length, into the evening, about the times and about the condition of the Republic, which had drawn them into shared reflection. In that conversation, Cotta would later report, many things were spoken with an almost prophetic clarity and spoken with such grief and foresight that it seemed nothing ill would later befall the Republic that had not already been foreseen as imminent.

Yet, once that entire conversation had come to its end, Crassus displayed such Human-Warmth, such Civility and Graciousness, that when they reclined for dinner, all the prior gloom of their speech seemed lifted. There was in Crassus a certain charm, a cultivated delight in Jesting (iucunditas) - that the day seemed not to have passed in a Remote-Villa, but inside the very Senate-House itself: so dignified was the Fellowship, and yet so light was the Conversation.

On the following day, once the elder Aristocratic-Men had rested, and all had come out to take a walk, Scaevola was said to have spoken first - after two or three turns along the garden paths. He said: "Why don't we imitate that Socrates of Plato's Phaedrus, Crassus? For this very plane tree of yours reminded me of it. Its wide-reaching branches shade this place no less fully than the one under which Socrates once rested - though, to me, that earlier tree seems to have grown more from Plato's Public-Speech than from the soil itself. And what Socrates did with such hardened feet - laying himself down on the grass so that he might speak words said to be Divinely-Inspired by Philosophy - surely such an act may be more justly permitted to my own feet."

To this, Crassus replied, "All the better indeed!" And it was said that he called for the slaves to bring cushions - and that all of them took their places on the seats beneath the plane tree.

VIII. Crassus: The Perfect Orator

Outside, inside Crassus' Villa at Tusculum, under the plane tree, on the cushions, and attended by slaves, their Minds had relaxed from the prior day's solemn discourse. As was his custom, Cotta recounted how Crassus had once offered a reflection on the pursuit of Public-Speech. Crassus had opened by saying that he did not believe Sulpicius and Cotta needed exhortation, but rather deserved the highest praise - for they had already attained such Capacity that they not only outshone their peers, but could be favorably compared to men of far greater Age and Experience.

"Indeed," Crassus said, "nothing seems to me more excellent than to be able - through Public-Speech - to bind together the gatherings of men, to attract their Minds, to direct their desires, and to lead them away from whatever binds them. This one thing - above all others - has always flourished in any Free People, and it has always held dominion most of all within Republics governed by Peace and Tranquility. For what could be more wondrous, than that - out of an Infinite-Crowd of Citizens, Plebs, and Women - one Aristocratic-Man alone, or only a few, should be able to accomplish by Public-Speech what Nature has offered to all? Or what could be more delightful, whether to witness or to hear, than a Structured-Speech shaped by Wise-Judgments and guided by pathways into the Kosmos - Harmonizing-Words, Well-Ordered and Well-Formed - Dignified, Polished, and Refined in expression?

"Or again, what could be more powerful, more majestic, than to sway the Movements of the People, the Scruples of Jurors, and the Gravity of the Senate - all through the Public-Speech of a single Aristocratic-Man? And what could be more Kingly, more worthy of a Free-Man, more Noble, than to offer aid to the supplicant's hand, raise up the fallen, bring safety to the endangered, deliver the threatened, and hold each citizen fast within the civic body? Or what could be more necessary than to possess the Arms of Speech - weapons by which one may shield oneself, challenge the wicked, or strike back when provoked?

"Come now, do not always confine your vision to the Forum, or the benches, the Rostra, and the Senate

House. What could be more fitting to Leisure-with-Dignity, or more proper to Human-Nature, than Aristocratic-Men engaged in Refined and Civil Conversation - Public-Speech that is never coarse in any matter? This alone distinguishes us from beasts: that we speak among ourselves, and through Public-Speech can express Inner-Movements and Sensations of our Minds.

"Who, then, would not rightly admire this power? Who would not labor to master it - so that in the very thing by which man surpasses beast, he might surpass even his fellow man? And if we turn now to even greater matters: What other force could ever have gathered scattered Humans into one place, drawn them out of Savage-Existence, and led them into Cultivation and Civil-Participation - into the Res Publica? Or, once Cities were Founded, what else could have established Laws, defined Judgments, and articulated Rights for Aristocratic-Men, plebs, and women?

"But not to pursue the nearly countless examples, I will express it in brief: It is through the Moderation and Wisdom of the Perfect Orator that not only his own dignity is preserved, but also the safety of many Private Citizens - and above all, of the entire Republic. Therefore, continue as you are, young Aristocratic-Men - and press with full effort into this study you have already begun. So that you may become a source of Honor to yourselves, an advantage to your friends, and a benefit to the Republic."

IX. Scaevola: Skeptical of Harmonizing-Words

Then Scaevola, with his usual graciousness, responded: "In the main, Crassus, I agree with your praise of Speech - and I do not deny either the Art or the glory of your father-in-law Laelius, nor of Antonius. But I must withhold agreement from two of your claims. First: that Orators were the founders and preservers of cities and of the Republic itself. Second: that the Orator, even outside the Forum and its Civic Institutions, holds dominion over every form of Speech and Human-Discourse."

He turned to Crassus and asked directly: "Who ever granted you that premise? Who would say that the Human-Race - once scattered among forests and mountains - was brought together not by the prudent judgment of Wise-Men, but by the tones of Harmonizing-Words delivered by smooth-speaking Eloquent-Men? Do you really believe that the Republic was constituted by Aristocratic-Men who merely spoke finely - men wrapped in Harmonizing-Words - rather than by those who governed through True-Counsel and Grave-Judgment?

"Romulus, the very founder of our city, gathered shepherds, formed alliances by marriage, and withstood military threats - not through ornamented Speech, but through singular Wisdom. Numa Pompilius, Servius Tullius, and the rest - did they leave behind dazzling

Oratory, or did they shape our city through thoughtful Rule? And even when the Kings were overthrown - was it not the Judgment of Lucius Brutus, and not his Eloquence, that turned the course of history?

"If I wished, I could list many examples of how Eloquent Men have done harm to the Republic. But I need only name the Gracchi. Tiberius and Gaius were supremely trained in the Art of Speech - but that very Eloquence, which you now praise as the Governing Art, led to division and disaster. Their father, though not particularly Eloquent, was prudent, dignified, and immensely useful to the Republic. By a single word and gesture, he reformed the tribal system and preserved civic stability. His sons, though Eloquent, shattered what he had secured."

He paused, then added with pointed clarity: "So forgive me, Crassus, if I hesitate to embrace the idea that Harmonizing-Words (ornatus) are the shaping force of Res Publica. You may call it Eloquence, but I see only the Outer-Adornment of Speech, and not the Inner-Structure of Counsel by which a Republic is truly governed."

X. Scaevola: Mustering an Army of Skeptics

Scaevola continued, courteous as always: "What of the Ancient Laws? The Customs of our Ancestors? The Auspices - those Sacred Signs by which you and I, Crassus, interpret the will of the gods and thereby safeguard the Res Publica? What of Religious Rites and Ceremonies? Or the Civil Laws - those same Laws that have been administered in my family for generations, without a trace of Eloquence? Were these things invented by Orators? Were they even understood by them - or ever claimed as part of their Art?"

He paused, then added: "Yes, I remember Servius Galba - a man Divine in Public-Speech - and Marcus Aemilius Porcina, and even Gaius Carbo, whom you, Crassus, defeated in your youth. Yet all were ignorant of Law, uncertain in Tradition, and untrained in Civil Knowledge. And aside from you, Crassus - who studied Civil Law not out of professional duty, but out of passion - who in our generation can make such a claim? The Orators of today? They are shamefully ignorant of the very Laws they presume to adorn with Speech. And now you assert - almost as if by right - that the Orator is Master of all forms of Discourse. But if we were not seated under your own plane tree, Crassus, if this were not your Domain, I would not allow such a claim to stand. I would summon many allies to challenge you, as if you had unlawfully seized possession of another's land.

"First would come the Pythagoreans, and the followers of Democritus - men with Harmonizing-Words in Speech and grave in wisdom - who would stake their claim over Natural Inquiry. You could not contest them, not even by sacred oath. Then the Philosophers would descend - those descended from Socrates himself. They would show that you know nothing of the Good or the Bad, of the Soul's Passions, of Ethics, or of Life rightly lived. They would prove that you have asked nothing, studied nothing, and grasped nothing.

"One by one, the sects would advance. The Academics would compel you to refute your every word. The Stoics would ensnare you in their nets of dialectic. The Peripatetics would reclaim even those very ornaments and devices of Speech you call your own - showing that Aristotle and Theophrastus had written more, and better, than all your rhetorical masters combined. And I will pass over the Mathematicians, Grammarians, and Musicians - whose Arts, frankly, share no kinship at all with your supposed Domain of Speech.

"Which is why I cannot support your extravagant claim, Crassus. Let this suffice - and it is already great: That inside the courts, the cause you defend appears more just. That inside the Assembly and the Senate, your words carry the greatest persuasive force. That among the Wise, you speak with Elegance - and among the Foolish, with the Appearance of Truth. If there is any man who can do more than this - it is not as an Orator. It is as you, Crassus: a singular Aristocratic-Man, possessed of a Private and Exceptional Power, not shared by the Common Faculty of Speech."

XI. Crassus: Rejects Plato's Gorgias

Then Crassus replied: "Scaevola, I am not unaware that these matters are often debated among the Greeks. When I returned from Macedonia as a quaestor, I visited Athens. At that time, the Academy was said to be flourishing - led by Charmadas, Clitomachus, and Aeschines. Metrodorus was also present, a man who had studied closely with them and had listened to Carneades himself, reputed to be the most piercing and copious speaker of his generation. Your own Panaetius had left behind his student, Mnesarchus. And among the Peripatetics were Critolaus and Diodorus - along with many others, all Noble and accomplished in Philosophy.

"But from all of them, I heard nearly the same thing: that the Orator should be barred from the helm of the Res Publica, exiled from the realm of Knowledge and Serious Matters, and confined instead to Courts and minor Assemblies - as if to a rhetorical millhouse, to grind out speeches like flour. I never agreed with them - nor even with Plato himself, the master and originator of such disputes, who, though mocking the Orators, seemed to me the greatest Orator of them all. While in Athens, I read his Gorgias with Charmadas. And in that very work, though he ridicules the Art of Speech, Plato seemed to me to practice it at its highest perfection.

"This, I believe, is a matter of terminology. The Greeks are more drawn to Contention than to Truth. If one defines an Orator as simply one who speaks fluently inside trials, before the people, or in the Senate - then even so, much must be granted. For, among citizens, plebs, and women, no one can move freely and effectively in such matters without deep experience in Civic-Life, knowledge of Laws and Customs, and insight into Human-Nature and Character. And if such knowledge is necessary to speak well in small matters, how could it possibly be absent in the greatest?

"But if someone insists that the Orator is only an Aristocratic-Man who speaks fluently, elegantly, and with abundance - then I ask: how could even that be achieved, unless he had already mastered the very things he speaks of? For the virtue of Speaking cannot arise unless the speaker has internalized the truths he expresses. Without that, there can be no true Eloquence - only empty Harmonizing-Words. So if Democritus the Physicist, as they say, spoke with grace, then the material came from Natural Science - but the style, the Harmonizing-Words, came from the Art of the Orator.

"If Plato, as I concede, spoke Divinely on subjects far removed from political life - and if Aristotle, Theophrastus, and Carneades expressed themselves with polish and power - then their subject matter may belong to other disciplines, but their Speech, their Public-

Speech, belongs to our Domain: the Domain of the Orator. For we also observe others - like Chrysippus, praised as the sharpest thinker - who spoke dryly and thinly on the very same subjects. Yet this did not diminish his status as a Philosopher. It simply shows that he lacked Harmonizing-Words, the verbal Art, which arises not from Philosophy but from Rhetoric, a distinct and noble Domain."

XII. Crassus: Inner Substance

Crassus continued: "So then - what is the true difference? How shall we distinguish the abundance and richness of those I have named, from the barrenness of those who do not employ such variety and elegance in Public-Speech? The True Orator will surely have this one mark: that his Speech is composed with Method, adorned with Harmonizing-Words, and shaped by a certain refinement and structure. But if the Speaker has not grasped, and the Orator does not truly understand, the subject matter - then the Speech must either not exist at all, or else become the target of ridicule as mere sound without sense. For what could be more absurd than a flow of even the most excellent and polished words, when no understanding lies beneath? Words, however fine, become madness when they lack the substance of Knowledge. Whatever the subject - whatever the field - if the Orator studies it as if it were a client's cause, he will speak on it more gracefully and persuasively than even its inventor or artisan. For though others may hold the technical knowledge, it is the Orator who gives it voice.

"If someone claims that there are certain causes or Domains proper only to the Orator - especially those bounded by the Law or situated inside the Forum - I will grant that our Art is most commonly exercised there. Yet even in those very fields, there are many things the so-called Rhetoricians neither teach nor understand. For who does not know that the greatest force of the Orator lies in moving Human-Minds - in stirring Citizens, plebs, and women to anger, hatred, or grief, and likewise in calming them toward gentleness and mercy? Unless the Orator has understood Human-Nature in full - the roots of our shared life and the causes by which Minds are incited or soothed - he will never be able to accomplish what he aims for in Speech.

"This, of course, seems to belong to the Philosophers. And rightly so. Let them hold the Knowledge of Things, if they desire to labor only there. But the Orator will lay rightful claim to the Domain of Speaking - a Domain which, without that knowledge, simply cannot exist. For this is the Orator's own: to speak with Weight and Refinement, in a manner fitted to the Shared-Sense and Soul of Humankind."

XIII. Crassus: Corner vs Full-Light

Crassus continued: "Scaevola, I freely acknowledge that Aristotle and Theophrastus wrote on these subjects. But take note: in this entire Domain, I claim nothing from them as borrowed. For in those matters which are shared - that is, those things which lie within the Common-Sphere of both Orator and Philosopher - I do not derive from them. Rather, even those Philosophers who dispute such matters concede that what is shared rightly belongs to the Orator as well. And so, those other books - apart from the ones they label 'Rhetorical' - they name and title under their own Art. But whenever these Philosopher-Men find themselves, as they often do, speaking on the Immortal Gods, on Piety, Concord, Friendship, the Common Rights of Citizens, Humanity, Nations, Justice, Equity, Moderation, Greatness of Soul, and every kind of Virtue - then, I suppose, the entire Gymnasium and all the Philosopher Schools will rise up in protest, crying that these matters are their exclusive Domain, and do not belong to the Orator at all.

"So be it. Let me grant them, if they please, this liberty: to speak - though only from some obscured interior of Knowledge, beneath the shelter of their Philosopher's-Corner - on such topics as they choose, within the confines of their Leisure-with-Dignity. But I will still reserve, and indeed I will lay claim to this for the

Orator: that he may give voice to these very same subjects - not with a pale and lifeless whisper in some shadowed portico, but with gravity and delight, and in the full light of Public-Speech.

"Indeed, I once held such discussions with the Philosophers while I was in Athens - urged on by Marcus Marcellus, who is now Curule Aedile. And were he not presently engaged in preparing the Games, he would be here with us today; for even then, as a young man, he was devoted to these studies with extraordinary zeal. And now, consider: when it comes to Lawgiving, to matters of War and Peace, to Alliances, Taxation, and the ordering of Civil Law - divided by class, rank, and age - let the Greeks, if they wish, prefer Lycurgus or Solon (though we count them among the Truly-Eloquent) to Hyperides or Demosthenes, those masters of the spoken word.

"Let them elevate our own Decemvirs - who composed the Twelve Tables and must certainly have been prudent men - above Servius Galba or your father-in-law, Gaius Laelius, though both were acknowledged to surpass others in the glory of Public-Speech. I will not deny that certain Arts rightly belong to those who have devoted their lives to them. But I will still affirm this: that the Orator - when full and perfected in his Art, and crowned with Harmonizing-Words - must be able to speak, with richness and variety, on every subject that belongs to the Shared-Life of the Republic."

XIV. Crassus: Rejects Socrates

Crassus continued: "For even in those very causes that all admit to be the Orator's Inner-Domain of Public-Speech, there often arises something that must be drawn up - not from forensic practice alone (which you say belongs exclusively to the Orator) - but from some deeper and more veiled chamber of knowledge, often hidden beneath the surface while facing the Philosopher's-Corner. Tell me, for example: can anyone provide Public-Speech either against or on behalf of a Military Commander without having entered into the structure of Military Affairs? Or can one do so without knowledge of the terrain - the geography of land and sea? Or when speaking to the Citizens, plebs, and women at the civic threshold about the passing or repeal of Laws, or inside the Senate about any matter concerning the framework of the Res Publica - is it possible to do so without a grounded Understanding and deep Prudence in Civil Affairs? And finally: can an Aristocratic-Man's Public-Speech even reach into the emotions and inner movements of the Soul - so as to ignite or subdue them (which is the very force that most defines the Orator) - without descending into the foundations where causes and explanations lie buried concerning Human-Nature and Moral Character, as taught by the Philosophers?

"I do not know whether this next claim will please you - but I will not hesitate to speak from where I stand: those fields you just named - Physics, Mathematics, and the other so-called Specialized Arts - belong indeed to those who dwell entirely within their vaulted Domains. But if someone wishes to bring forth these very Arts through Public-Speech, then he must first descend into them and then rise again - carrying them upward - by seeking refuge in the Orator's Capacity. For take the example of Philon the Architect, who built the arsenal for the Athenians. It is agreed that he laid open the reasoning of his design with great Eloquence before the People. But are we to think he spoke well because of his Art as an Architect, or because of his power as an Orator? Or again: suppose that I, Marcus Antonius, had been required to speak on behalf of Hermodorus concerning naval construction. After I had absorbed the structural cause from him, I could have delivered a polished and abundant Public-Speech on a technical Art that was not my own.

"And as for Asclepiades, that physician and friend of ours - when he surpassed all other doctors in Eloquence, was it by the power of Medicine that he spoke with refined Speech? No - it was by the power of Public-Speech. And this shows that the saying of Socrates - that 'All men are sufficiently Eloquent in what they know' - though plausible, is not true. No, the truth is this: No one can speak with Eloquence on what he does not understand. But even if he understands it perfectly, if he is ignorant of how to shape and elevate his words, he will never speak with Eloquence about the very thing he knows."

XV. Crassus: Power of Harmonizing-Words

Crassus continued: "Therefore, if some Aristocratic-Man wishes to grasp and define the full and proper power of the Orator, I believe such a Man - worthy of so weighty a name - will be this: one who, in whatever matter may arise that requires Public-Speech, can speak with Prudence, Structure, Ornament, Memory - and with a certain Dignity in his Physical Delivery. Now, if that seems too infinite to anyone - this 'Whatever Matter May Arise' notion - then let them, if they wish, cut and prune it down to their liking. But even so, I will still hold to this: Even if the Orator is ignorant of those matters that lie in other Fields of Knowledge, and is only well-versed in the disputes and practices of Forensic Speech - still, if he must speak on such matters, once he has learned from those who dwell in that Field, he will speak far better as an Orator than those same Experts who actually practice the Art.

"For instance, if a matter arises in Military Affairs, and Sulpicius must speak on it - he will consult our kinsman, Gaius Marius. And after receiving the substance from him, he will deliver his Speech so clearly and richly that Marius himself may seem to Understand those matters more fully through the Orator's expression than through his own Experience.

"If the subject is Civil Law, the Orator will confer with you, Scaevola - and even though you are the most Prudent and Skilled in that Field, the Orator, having taken in the material from you, will surpass you in the Art of Speaking.

"And if the case touches on Human-Nature - on Vices, Desires, Restraint, Suffering, or Death - then, if the Orator sees fit (though he ought already to have internalized such things), he may consult with Sextus Pompeius, a man well trained in Philosophy. But without question, whatever Domain of Speech the Orator reclaims from another Field, he will express it with Harmonizing-Words and far more Elegance than the very one who taught it to him.

"Still, if you will listen to me: since Philosophy has been divided into three branches - (1) the deep obscurities of Nature, (2) the sharp logic of Argument, and (3) the conduct of Life and Character - let us leave aside the first two, and grant them as concessions to our own practical limitations. But the third - the one that has always belonged to the Orator's Domain - if we do not hold to it, we leave the Orator with nothing in which he can truly become great.

"For this reason, the whole Field of Life and Character must be thoroughly explored and absorbed by the Orator. As for the rest - even if he does not master it - he will still be able to elevate it with Ornamental-Speech, once it has passed into his keeping and has been committed to his Understanding."

XVI. The Orator and the Arts

Crassus continued: "For indeed, if it is accepted among the learned that Aratus - though ignorant of astronomy - used Harmonizing-Words when he spoke of the heavens and stars in the Most-Excellent verse; and that Nicander of Colophon - though far removed from rustic life - wrote superbly on agricultural matters, not by rustic skill, but by a certain poetic Art - then why should the Orator not speak with the highest Eloquence on those matters which he has come to know for a specific cause and at a specific time?

"For the Orator is closely allied to the Poet: the Poet is bound by meter more strictly, while the Orator is freer in his choice of words. Yet in many forms of Harmonizing-Words, they are companions - nearly equals. In one way especially, they are alike: neither is confined by fixed boundaries or rigid definitions, but may move freely across the Fields of Thought with the full abundance of their Capacity.

"And so, Scaevola - when you said that you would not have tolerated my earlier claim (except that you were, as it were, dwelling for a time within my Domain) - that in every kind of discourse, in every region of Shared-Humanity, the Orator ought to be perfected:

"I swear, I would never have said such a thing if I believed the Orator I was imagining to be me.

"But - I hold the same view as Gaius Lucilius, that sharp and witty man, who once said (though he was never especially friendly toward me, perhaps because of this very topic) - still, he was learned and urbane: 'No one should be counted among the number of Orators unless he has been thoroughly cultivated in all the Arts that are worthy of a Free-Man. Even if these Arts are not explicitly summoned into Speech, it becomes clear - immediately - whether one has been shaped by them, or remains altogether ignorant.'

"Just like those who play ball: they do not use the specific forms of the wrestling-school in the game itself, yet their movements make it obvious whether they have trained in the gymnasium. Likewise, someone forming a sculpture - though his Act may not involve painting - will still reveal whether he knows how to paint or is completely untrained.

"In the same way, in our Speeches - whether inside the Courts, the Assemblies, or the Senate - even if the other Liberal Arts are not overtly gathered and displayed, it becomes readily apparent whether the speaker is performing with the shallow gestures of schoolboy declamation, or whether he approaches Public-Speech fortified by the full education of a Free-Born Soul raised for the Shared Life of the Republic."

XVII. A Concession and a Second Disclaimer

Scaevola replied with a smile: "I shall no longer struggle with you, Crassus. For you have, by a kind of rhetorical sleight-of-hand, accomplished exactly what you intended: you conceded what I insisted did not belong to the Orator - only to turn it once more and return it to him as his own Rightful-Domain.

"When I served as praetor and came to Rhodes, I held discussions with that famous teacher of the discipline - Apollonius - and I compared with him the doctrines I had taken in from Panaetius. He mocked them, as he was wont to do - mocked Philosophy itself - looked down upon it, and spoke not gravely but with polished contempt.

"But your way of speaking, Crassus, was of another kind altogether. You mocked no Art, no Discipline. Rather, you gathered them all into a noble procession - companions and attendants in the triumphal march of the Orator."

"And so," he continued, "if there were a Man who could unite all these Arts within himself - binding them into one - and if he could also join to them the commanding Power of Public-Speech adorned with Ornamental-Wisdom, I could not deny that such a Man would be rare and awe-inspiring. And if such a Man ever lived - or ever could live - it would surely be you, Crassus. In my own judgment - and I say this with due respect to these others - you have left scarcely any praise unclaimed that rightfully belongs to the greatest Orators.

"And yet, even if you lack nothing that pertains to Action and Speech within the Res Publica, perhaps you have ascribed too much to that Knowledge which you say belongs to the Orator. Tell me - do you not attribute more to him than either the Facts or the Truth can bear?"

To this, Crassus responded: "Remember - I was not speaking of myself, but of the Power that belongs to the Orator.

"What have we learned? What could we have possibly Known - we who were summoned to Action before we were ever guided to Understanding? The Forum seized us before the Schools had shaped us. We breathed in Ambition before we had even exhaled a single breath of Meditation. The Res Publica and the burdens of our Aristocratic Allies laid claim to our labor before the Soul had time to sense the magnitude of its task.

"So if you believe that even we - deprived of Dedicated-Leisure, of Formal-Learning, and, though you may grant us Natural-Talent, deprived too of the burning hunger to Know - have still managed something: then imagine what might become of one whose Natural-Endowment is greater still, and who possesses all those resources I never touched. What kind of Orator - what Greatness - might emerge from such a Soul?"

XVIII. Public-Speaking and Craftsmen

Then Antonius said: "Crassus, I am persuaded by what you've said. I do not doubt that the Orator would speak far more abundantly in Public-Speech if he truly grasped the Reason and Nature of all Domains and Arts.

"But first - it is exceedingly difficult to do, especially in our own kind of Aristocratic Life: freed, yes, from the burdens of the animal laborens, but constantly drawn into the unceasing demands of our Public Roles.

"Second, I fear this: that we might be pulled away from the daily discipline and popular exercise of Public-Speaking as it belongs to the Forum and to the People.

"For there is, in my Mind, one kind of Speech that belongs to the Men you just mentioned - those who, even if they speak with gravity and with Harmonizing-Words about Nature or Human Matters, still speak in a manner smooth, polished, and gleaming - more suited to the Gymnasium and to the sheen of wrestling oil than to the dust, din, and hard-edges of Civic Life and the inside of the Forum.

"For myself - though I came late and lightly to Greek Letters - when I departed for Cilicia as Proconsul and arrived in Athens, I was detained many days by the season. During that time, I kept company with many learned men - most of the very ones you just now named.

"And somehow word had spread that I, like you, often dealt with Major Causes. So, one by one, each of them tried - as best he could - to debate the Role and Art of the Orator.

Mnesarchus - that very same man - declared that the ones we call Orators are mere Craftsmen: quick tongues, trained in repetition. For him, no one could be an Orator unless he were a True Sage. Eloquence itself, he said, was a kind of Virtue, since it derived from the Science of Speaking Well. And since all Virtues are equal, he argued, anyone who possessed Eloquence must therefore possess them all - and so be Wise.

"But that was a prickly, narrow, and brittle sort of Speech - far removed from the Forum's Republican-Sensibilities, and even farther from the Roman rhythm of Public-Speaking itself.

"Charmadas, by contrast, spoke on the same matters with far more richness. He did not reveal his own position - for that was the inherited custom of the Academy, always to contradict in argument - but he made clear what he believed: that those called Rhetoricians, and those who handed down Rules for Speaking, truly

Grasped nothing at all. In his view, no one could ever attain the Faculty of Public-Speech unless he had studied the deep discoveries of the Philosophers."

XIX. Public-Speaking and Menedemus' Wisdom

"Yet there were articulate men - Athenian Citizens - who had themselves been deeply engaged in the life of the Res Publica and in Real Causes, and who offered a powerful counterargument. Chief among them was Menedemus, recently in Rome and a guest in my own home. He argued that there exists a kind of Civic-Wisdom: a Capacity devoted to grasping and shaping the Rational-Structure by which Republics are Founded, Ordered, and Sustained. He was a vigorous man, overflowing with Learning, and equipped with astonishing diversity and depth of Knowledge.

"He insisted that every element of this Civic-Wisdom must be sought within Philosophy. The matters requiring Judgment in the Res Publica - concerning the Immortal Gods, the Formation of Youth, Justice, Endurance, Moderation, the Harmonious-Proportion of All Things, and all that without which Cities cannot endure, or at least cannot be Morally Well-Ordered - were nowhere to be found, he said, among the teachings of the so-called Rhetoricians.

"And so, he would ask: 'If these Teachers of Public-Speech claim their Art embraces the most serious

Human-Concerns, why then are their books filled with trivialities - Prologues, Epilogues, stylistic ornaments - while remaining wholly silent on the Founding of Cities, the Writing of Laws, and the cultivation of Civic Virtues such as Justice, Equity, Trustworthiness, the Restraining of Desires, and the Shaping of Human-Character?'

"Indeed," Antonius added, "he would often mock their Rules of Rhetoric - not merely because they lacked Civic-Wisdom, but because they failed even to understand the deeper Method and Harmonizing-Pathway of Public-Speaking.

"For he held that the first and most essential task of the Orator is this: 'To Appear - within the Minds of those he addresses - as the very kind of Man he himself desires to be seen as. And that Effect arises not from Technique, but from the Dignity of one's Life.' Yet on this point, those Rhetorical Teachers remained wholly silent.

"Second: 'The Minds of one's Hearers must be stirred - precisely, and in the direction the Orator intends. But such movement cannot occur unless the Speaker understands the inward forces that sway Human-Minds: what Emotions, what Apprehensions, what Rhythm of Harmonizing-Words carry them forward. And these lie hidden within the Core of Philosophy - buried in obscurity, far beyond the reach of those who merely polish the surface of Speech.'

"Menedemus did not rely on logic alone, but proved his argument by examples. From Memory, he would recite long passages from the Structured-Speeches of Demosthenes - showing how, in stirring the Minds of Jurors, Citizens, Plebs, and Women, Demosthenes had clearly grasped the inner Causes of those Effects. And so he concluded: 'Such knowledge does not belong to Philosophers alone - but is essential to the True Orator.'"

XX. Continued Wisdom from Menedemus

Antonius continued: "To these claims, our Athenian guest Menedemus would often reply: 'I do not deny that Demosthenes possessed the highest Civic-Wisdom and the most extraordinary power in Public-Speaking. Whether this arose from natural Genius or - as is widely believed - through his eager study under Plato does not concern me. What matters,' he would insist, 'is not what Demosthenes became, but what these Teachers of Rhetoric are actually capable of Teaching.'

"He frequently pressed his argument toward this conclusion: 'There is, in truth, no genuine Art of Public-Speaking at all.'

"Then he would offer his reasoning: 'We are born already possessing the Capacities that Orators perform. By Nature, we know how to flatter and to supplicate those from whom we seek something. We know how to threaten and to frighten our adversaries. We can recount past actions, affirm intent, undermine the claims of others, and, finally, plead, lament, and cry out in protest.'

"'These,' he would say, 'are the fundamental Elements of Public-Speaking. And they do not arise from Art, but from Natural-Capacity, refined through Habit and Practice - through the urgency of Experience and the sharpening of Apprehension.'

"To support his case, Menedemus drew upon history. He pointed out that none of the early writers on Rhetoric - not even its so-called inventors, Corax and Tisias - were known for actual Eloquence. And yet, he said, countless men had become powerful Speakers without ever studying Rhetoric or caring to learn it.

"He even added - whether jesting or in earnest - that I myself had never studied the Art of Rhetoric, and yet seemed to possess, as he put it, some power in Public-Speech. On the first point, I freely agreed: I never studied their Art. On the second - that I nevertheless Speak effectively - I thought he was either misjudging me or making sport.

"Menedemus went further: 'No true Art exists unless it is founded upon certain and stable Knowledge - on grasped, unwavering Principles, aimed at a single, reliable Outcome. But everything the Orator handles is unstable and indefinite. The Speaker often does not truly understand what he says. And the Hearers receive not

Knowledge, but fleeting, confused, or deceptive Opinion.'

"In short, he seemed wholly resolved to convince me that there is no Art of Public-Speaking - and that no one can speak with true fullness or depth unless he has internalized the Structured-Teachings of the most learned Philosophers.

"And in truth," Antonius added with a half-smile, "Charmadas once remarked - when admiring your Genius, Crassus - that I seemed easily persuaded in listening, while you, in every discussion, stood firm in resistance."

XXI. Antonius' Treatise and Sulpicius' Interjection

Antonius continued: "And so, compelled by this very conviction, I once composed a brief Treatise - one that slipped from my hands without my knowledge or consent and made its way into the Public-Sphere. In it, I confessed that while I had known many who were Skilled-in-Speaking, I had yet to encounter anyone I would truly call Eloquent.

"For I defined as Skilled-in-Speaking the man who could express himself with sharpness and clarity, speaking from within the Domain of Shared-Opinion in front of citizens, plebs, and women. But I reserved the title Eloquent for that man who could seem to elevate and magnify whatever he touched - one who could Embellish,

Amplify, and Adorn each subject with a wondrous power that entered into every recess of the topic, drawing up from within himself the summit-source - the Wellspring - of every resource belonging to Public-Speech.

"Now if we ourselves fall short of such heights - because, before ever ascending into study, we were already pulled downward by ambition and thrown into the dust of the Forum - this failure lies not within the nature of Oratory itself, but within the course our lives have taken.

"Yet I see no cause to bury myself in despair. For, judging by the natural powers I have seen among our Roman Aristocratic-Men, I believe one will yet appear - someone endowed with greater eagerness for study than we have shown, liberated from the burdens of animal laborens, and blessed with time, resources, and the will to learn. Such a man, armed with greater perseverance and discipline, who devotes himself fully to Listening, Reading, and Writing, will at last rise to become the kind of Orator we have long imagined. And that man, I say, will deserve the name not merely Skilled, but truly Eloquent.

"Perhaps Crassus already fulfills that vision. Or, if another should come - one who, though equal in talent, surpasses Crassus in breadth of study, in attentive listening, and in careful writing - he may add something more. But only a little."

At this point, Sulpicius interjected: "This is a rare fortune for both me and Cotta, Crassus - one we scarcely dared to hope for. When we came here, we were content to listen at a distance, happy even if your conversations drifted to other matters. But now, you have drawn us directly into the very interior-space of this whole Practice - this Domain of Study, of Art, and of Power-in-Public-Speech. It surpasses anything we might have dreamed.

"As for myself, I have long burned with the desire to learn from both of you - especially from you, Crassus, whom I have loved dearly since boyhood and never willingly left. And yet, despite my nearness to you, I have never been able to draw from you a single word about the Force or Method of Public-Speaking - no matter how often I asked directly, or even sought help from Drusus.

"You, Antonius - if I may speak plainly - have never failed to answer me. Often, you have taught me the very paths you take when you speak.

"And now, since both of you have opened the gateway to the knowledge we seek - and since Crassus was the first to step through - grant us this favor: to pursue, with full clarity and subtlety, all that you believe about the entire Domain of Public-Speech.

"If we can receive this from you, Crassus, I will count it as a lasting debt - not only to this Palaestra and your Villa here in Tusculum - but I will hold your

Gymnasium to be greater than even the famed Academy of Plato or the Lyceum of Aristotle."

XXII. Crassus Answers Questions and Mocks Greeks

Then Crassus replied: "On the contrary, Sulpicius - let us begin with Antonius. He both can do what you ask and, as I gather from you, is accustomed to doing it. As for myself, I must confess: I have always avoided this kind of inquiry altogether. And as you just said, even when you pressed me with eagerness, I consistently declined.

"But I never refused out of arrogance or contempt, nor out of reluctance to support your pursuit - a pursuit that is wholly Noble and Right. For I have long believed that among all Aristocratic-Men, you are the one most Naturally-Born and inwardly shaped for Public-Speech. No - my hesitation came from elsewhere: my lack of practice in this Academic kind of Discussion, and my unfamiliarity with those matters handed down, as if by Art."

At this, Cotta joined in: "Well then, since we've already passed the hardest hurdle - getting you, Crassus, to speak - if you now leave our questions unanswered, the fault will lie with us, not with you."

Crassus smiled: "On these matters, then, I will respond - as it is written in wills and legal declarations - 'as far as I know and am able.'"

Antonius added: "And truly - what you do not know or cannot do - who among us would dare claim he could?"

Crassus replied: "Well then - under this one condition: that I may say 'I do not know' when I do not, and 'I cannot' when I cannot - ask what you will." Then Sulpicius began: "Very well, let us begin with what Antonius has already raised. Do you believe there truly exists such a thing as an Art of Speaking?"

Crassus, with a half-smile, replied: "What's this? You examine me as though I were some idle little Greek - a loquacious fellow, well-read perhaps, and eager to offer his private opinion on some abstract proposition!

"Tell me - when do you suppose I ever studied or even considered such things? Have I not always mocked the sheer audacity of those men who, seated in their lecture halls, invite passersby from the crowd to pose questions on any subject whatever?

"Gorgias of Leontini, they say, was the first to do this - he who seemed to promise something great and bold when he claimed he was ready to speak about anything a man might ask. But over time, this became commonplace. Even today, such men claim there is no subject so vast, no question so sudden or strange, that they cannot lay out everything that could possibly be said about it.

"If I had thought, Cotta - or you, Sulpicius - that this was what you wished to hear, I would have brought along some Greek who delights in such disputations. And that would not have been difficult. For at present, staying with Marcus Piso, there is a young man already devoted to this very pursuit - sharp in mind, enthusiastic for our traditions - a certain Peripatetic named Staseas. He is well known to me. And from what I hear among the masters of his school, he is ranked among their most eminent voices."

XXIII. Scaevola Calls Crassus a God

Then Scaevola interjected: "And who is this Staseas you mention to me, Crassus - this Peripatetic? You must learn to yield to the desires of the young. They are not seeking the idle chatter of some Greek, babbling daily with no relevance to the Res Publica, nor are they asking for a singsong lesson lifted from the schoolroom. They seek the wisdom of a man deemed supreme in both Judgment and Speech - one tested in the gravest of causes, and within this very dwelling-place of Roman Power and Glory. They desire to follow in your footsteps. They seek your iudicium.

"For my part," Scaevola continued, "I have always believed you something of a god when you speak - but beyond your Public-Speech, I most admire your Humanity. And now, Crassus, it is precisely this quality you must display: do not withdraw from the Inquiry these young men so eagerly pursue."

Crassus replied: "I am willing - and I will not hesitate to offer, briefly and in my own way, what I think about each matter. And first, since I do not believe I can ignore your authority, Scaevola, I'll begin by saying this: to me, Public-Speech is either no Art at all - or else a very slender one. But I believe that the entire dispute among learned men on this point is a quarrel over words, not substance.

"For if Art is defined - just as Antonius outlined earlier - as something based on clearly grasped and fully examined matters, detached from the world of shifting opinion, and held together by certain knowledge, then I do not believe Public-Speech qualifies as an Art. The reason is this: everything in our Forum-Speech is variable, unstable, and oriented toward the rough Understanding of citizens, plebs, and women - the ever-fluctuating judgments of the Crowd.

"But if, instead, we speak of Rules - not formal definitions, but the observations and reflections of skilled and experienced men - Rules that have been shaped by long Practice, named and illustrated by Examples, arranged in ordered Parts: then I see no reason why, even if not a full-fledged Art in the strict sense of Philosophy, it might still be rightly called an Art by the standards of Common-Sense.

"Still, whether it is truly an Art, or only something resembling one - it must not be dismissed. But we must recognize this: there are greater and deeper forces at work in the shaping of true Eloquence."

XXIV. Crassus Begins Providing Rules on Speaking

Then Antonius, with genuine conviction, affirmed his agreement - not because Crassus had taken up the Art of Speaking in the manner of those who would confine the whole force of Public Speech within the narrow bounds of technical instruction, nor like those Philosophers who cast it aside entirely.

"But I do think, Crassus," he said, "that you'd be doing these young men a real kindness - if you would now unfold those things which you believe help more in Speaking than the Art itself."

"I will speak," replied Crassus, "since I've begun. And I ask only this of you: do not betray these Deliriums of mine. I'll temper myself, though, so that I don't seem like a teacher or technician - but more like one of those citizens in the toga, a man of the Republic, one who's lived in Public life, with practice but without pretense. Let it seem not that I've delivered some finished Art, but that I just happened to fall, by chance, into this conversation of yours."

He continued: "When I was campaigning for office, I'd always send Scaevola away when I went to canvass the citizens - the plebs and even the women! I'd say I wanted the Freedom to be Foolish. For there's no such thing as Persuasion without Flattery, and no Flattery - done well - that isn't also Foolish. And among all men, he's the last in whose presence I'd want to be seen as a Fool. Yet as Fortune would have it, he now stands here, both witness and judge to my Foolishness."

"For what," he said, "is more Foolish than to speak about Speaking - when even Speaking itself is never Not-Foolish, except when it becomes Absolutely Necessary?"

"Continue, Crassus," said Mucius. "That shame you fear - I'll take it upon myself and guarantee your honor."

XXV. Natural-Capacity and the Limits of Public-Speaking

"And so," said Crassus, "this is how I see it: Nature - and Natural-Capacity - are the first and greatest Forces behind the power of Speaking. Those Writers of the Art whom Antonius mentioned earlier did not lack Rules or Methods; what they lacked was Nature itself.

"For within the Soul and Mind, there must be agile and fiery Movements - sharp for Invention, full and flowing for Expression and Harmonizing, and steady for Memory. Whoever believes that these traits can be taught through Art is deeply mistaken. For if Instruction could truly ignite these Inner-Fires and stir such Motion, that would be a wondrous thing indeed. But such Movements are gifts of Nature; they cannot be kindled or set in motion by Art.

"And what of those other Qualities - given at birth along with the Human-Being itself? The looseness and flexibility of the tongue, the tone and range of voice, the breadth of chest, the strength and endurance of the whole body, and the very symmetry of one's face and frame?

"I do not say this to deny the power of Art to refine - but to place its role rightly. Even what is already good can be perfected, and what is lacking may still be sharpened or corrected. Yet there are some whose tongues are tied, whose voices are grating, whose gestures and expressions are so unruly and grotesque, that even with the strength of both Genius and Method, they cannot rise to the rank of a true Orator. While others are so finely formed, so adorned by Nature's gifts, that they seem not born, but crafted by Divine hands.

"To take on the Role of the Orator is no small thing - it is a heavy burden, almost a Divine Commission: to stand alone, with all others silent, and speak before the Assembly of Citizens on the most serious affairs of the Res Publica. In such moments, every eye and ear is tuned to fault. And whatever blemish is perceived - however slight - it clouds the praise and dims the light of what is admirable.

"Yet I say none of this to discourage young Aristocratic-Men from the pursuit of Public-Speech merely because they lack some singular Natural-

Advantage. Who does not see that Gaius Coelius - though modest in his talent - still rose to great honor in the Republic? And who among you does not recognize that Quintus Varius - rugged, unrefined, and coarse - has nevertheless won the favor of citizens, plebs, and women alike, through the sheer power of Speaking, such as it is?"

XXVI. The Res Publica Ideal: Public-Speech and Shame

"But since our inquiry concerns the Orator," Crassus continued, "we must now shape, in words, a figure refined of every fault and adorned with every form of Virtue - an image of the Ideal. For even though the sheer flood of lawsuits, the clamor of causes, and the rugged chaos of the Forum may offer room for even the most flawed of Speakers, still, we must not let go of our pursuit of the Res Publica Ideal.

"Consider those Practices," he said, "in which the aim is not Utility or Necessity, but the free Delight of the Mind - how exacting, how almost disdainful, is our Judgment! In those Domains, there are no lawsuits, no compulsory quarrels, no citizen forced to endure what is crude or misshapen - as they must in the Forum. No one must tolerate a poor Actor in the Theater; yet the same cannot be said of the Courts.

"Therefore, the Orator must shape himself not merely to satisfy those who have no choice but to hear him, but to appear Admirable to those who are free to

Judge. And if you ask me openly," Crassus said, casting his eyes across the group, "I shall now speak - among friends - what I have long held silently and always believed unfit for Public speech.

"Even those who Speak best - who carry it with the greatest grace and power - if they approach their task without hesitation, without the slightest Visible-Disturbance at the beginning of their Speech, appear to me almost Shameless. And yet, I hold this to be natural. For the more fully a man grasps what Speaking is, the more he feels its weight, the hidden perils of outcome, and the immense expectation of those listening.

"But the one who cannot bring forth anything worthy - of the cause, of the Assembly, of the very name of Orator - and yet trembles nonetheless, seems no less Shameless. For it is not the mere sensation of Shame that guards against Disgrace - it is the refusal to speak unworthily that protects one's Dignity. And those who feel no Shame at all - which I observe in far too many - deserve not just blame, but, I dare say, punishment.

"For myself," he added, "I observe this even in you - and most of all in myself: I pale at the start of every Speech. My whole body trembles, and my very Soul quakes. I remember, in my youth, when I rose to prosecute for the first time - I was so overcome by fear that I owed my deliverance to Quintus Maximus, who, seeing me shattered with terror, dismissed the trial at once."

At this, the entire circle nodded and murmured in agreement - for in Crassus, there was a kind of Miraculous-Shame, a noble restraint that did not hinder his Speaking, but rather magnified his Authority through the very image of Uprightness.

XXVII. Public-Speech and Reputational Fear

Then Antonius spoke: "I have often observed what you describe, Crassus - not only in you, but in all the greatest Orators - though in my judgment, none has ever equaled your measure. I have seen the disturbance in you, visible at the opening of a Public-Speech, as if your whole Soul were being summoned into Judgment.

"I used to wonder why it was that the very Aristocratic-Men most gifted in Speaking seemed to be those who feared it most. And I have come to believe the cause lies in two truths.

"The first is this: those trained by both Nature and Practice know full well that even the greatest Orators cannot always achieve what they intend. And so, each time they rise to Speak, they do so with the Memory of past defeats - and with the living fear that failure, having once occurred, may rise again.

"The second reason," Antonius continued, "is one I confess often weighs upon me. In every other Art, when a practitioner of proven excellence performs below expectation, the cause is thought to be Circumstance - perhaps fatigue or illness. 'Roscius chose not to perform today,' they say. Or, 'He was unwell.' But when an Orator stumbles - even once - it is never forgiven as momentary misfortune. It is marked as Stupidity.

"And Stupidity, unlike fatigue or illness, cannot be excused. It is taken not as a slip, but as a stain upon the man himself - a revelation of his True Capacity.

"That is why, in Public-Speech, we face the harshest tribunal. Each time we rise, we are placed on Trial. The Actor may misstep and still be thought skillful. But the Orator who falters only once earns - whether rightly or not - a Reputation for slowness, dullness, and unfitness for the Assembly. And that stain lingers, long after the words are forgotten."

XXVIII. Crassus Points to the Method of Roscius the Actor

Young Antonius resumed: "That point you made, Crassus - that many things required by an Orator must come from Nature, and cannot be supplied by teaching - I agree with most strongly. And on that very point, I most admired the great teacher Apollonius of Alabanda. Though he taught for a fee, he would never allow his students to waste their time with him if he judged they could not become Orators. He would dismiss them - and guide each student instead toward the Art he thought best suited to their Nature.

"For most other Arts," Antonius continued, "it is enough merely to resemble the practitioner. The craft can be passed down, even hammered in through repetition if a student is slow to grasp it, and retained through Memory. One does not need a quick tongue, nor verbal speed, nor - finally - any of those things which lie beyond our control: appearance, expression, voice.

"But in the Orator," he said, "we require the sharpness of the Dialectician, the insight of the Philosopher, the words of the Poet, the Memory of the Jurist, the voice of the Tragedian, and the gesture of the greatest Actor. For this reason, there is no rarer creature among humans than the Perfect Orator. In every other Art, a person is praised if he attains even moderate skill in a single Domain. But in Oratory, unless a man possesses the highest excellence in every Domain, he cannot win approval."

At this, Crassus replied: "Just consider," he said, "how in even the lightest and most trivial Arts, people apply more discipline and rigor than in this one - which we all agree to be the greatest.

"I often hear Roscius say that he has yet to find a single pupil he truly approves of - not because there are no capable students, but because he cannot tolerate even the smallest flaw. Nothing leaves such a lasting impression - nothing is so sharply etched into Memory - as the Thing that Offends in a performance.

"So, if we direct our praise of the Orator by analogy to Roscius the Actor, you can see what is required: nothing must be done unless it is perfect, unless it is carried out with Highest-Grace, unless it is Fully-Proper, and capable of Moving and Delighting all.

"This is why," Crassus added, "we now call anyone who excels in his field the 'Roscius' of that profession. And it is this Completeness - this Perfection - I desire in an Orator. I myself am far from it, and I say so boldly. I ask that you pardon me - but I do not pardon others. For anyone who cannot do it, who performs with defect, or whose very nature is unfit for the task - I believe, with Apollonius, that he must be redirected toward the kind of work he can perform."

XXIX. Crassus Asks to Speak in the Roman Manner

Sulpicius then said, smiling: "What then? Do you advise me - and this companion Cotta here - to abandon Public-Speaking and instead study Civil Law or Military Strategy? For who, indeed, could ever attain to that summit you described - perfection in every form and kind?"

Crassus replied: "Not at all. On the contrary, because I have recognized in both of you an extraordinary and radiant Natural-Endowment for

Speaking, I presented these things. I shaped my whole Speech not to deter those who cannot attain - but to sharpen and inspire those, like you, who can.

"And though I have seen clearly in both of you a remarkable Genius and Determination, still, those qualities which I described - perhaps at greater length than even the Greeks typically do - are, in your case, Sulpicius, nothing short of Divine.

"For I do not believe I have ever heard anyone more perfectly shaped for Speaking - whether in bodily movement, posture, natural presence, or voice. Your voice is both full and pleasing. Now, for those to whom Nature grants less in these areas, it is still possible to reach a high level - provided they make moderate and skilled use of the gifts they do have, and above all, avoid anything improper or unfitting.

"This," he said, "is what must be guarded against most - and about which it is most difficult to give reliable instruction. Not just for me, who Speaks as a kind of householder in these matters, but even for Roscius himself. I've often heard him say that the Essence of his Art is Propriety - that one must always be Becoming. And yet, this one thing, he says, cannot be taught by any Art."

Then Crassus paused and added with a smile: "But if it pleases you, let us now shift the conversation elsewhere - and speak for a while, in our Roman manner, not in this Rhetorical mode."

"Not in the least!" cried Cotta. "You will do no such thing! We now demand - yes, demand - that since you have kept us so tightly bound to this study and have refused to let us stray to any other Art, you must now explain to us whatever it is that you yourself possess in Speaking.

"We're not asking for too much. We're satisfied with that humble eloquence of yours. We only ask - so that we may not fall too far short - that you show us what you have attained in Speaking. You've said that Nature has not withheld too much from us - so tell us, what must be added to what we already have?"

XXX. Crassus Discuss His Method (Not His Art)

Then Crassus, smiling, replied: "What do you suppose the answer is, Cotta, if not this: a burning passion - a kind of deep and persistent Loving-Fire? Without that, nothing great has ever been achieved in life; and most certainly, no one has ever attained what you seek without it. But truthfully, I don't see that you need to be urged toward this. You're already quite troublesome to me as it is - so eager are you, so inflamed with desire for this very pursuit!

"Still, passion alone is not enough. Passion cannot carry anyone to their destination unless they also know the road that leads to it. That path - the one that draws and guides toward the goal - must be understood.

"So then," Crassus continued, "since the burden you're placing on me is somewhat lighter - since you're not asking for a Grand-Discourse on the Art of the Orator, but only to hear something of my own Method, such as it is - I will lay it out. It's not particularly obscure, nor especially difficult, nor lofty, nor weighty. I will simply describe a certain manner of Daily-Habit - a Rhythm I once followed back when, as a young man, I had the freedom to immerse myself in this study."

At that, Sulpicius exclaimed: "O Cotta, what a day we've received! This is the moment we long hoped for. No amount of pleading, or scheming, or subtle observation ever allowed me to learn what it was that Crassus actually did - what he practiced in preparation for Speaking.

"I could only guess at it - maybe catching glimpses in the way he moved, or from his Greek secretary and reader, Diphilus. But now, I believe we have at last achieved what we desired. And soon, we shall finally hear, straight from Crassus himself, all the things we've long hungered to understand."

XXXI. Speaking Methods: Common and Worn-Down Precepts

Then Crassus said: "But truly, Sulpicius, I suspect that once you've heard what I have to say, you'll be less inclined to admire it than to wonder why you ever wanted to hear it in the first place. For nothing I shall say is obscure, nothing will live up to your high expectations, nothing will strike you as unheard-of or new to anyone.

"To begin with, I will not deny that I studied the Common and Worn-Down Precepts - those Maxims that belong to any Aristocratic-Man raised with even a modest Liberal-Education. That, for example, the first duty of the Orator is to Speak in a way suited to Persuading (***should we put citizens, plebs, and women*****). And that every Structured-Speech falls into one of two basic Forms: either a question posed about an Indeterminate Matter - without any fixed Person or Time - or a question that concerns some Definite Matter, situated within a specific Person and Time.

"In either Form," Crassus continued, "whatever point of controversy arises is typically directed to one of several types of Inquiry: whether something happened; what kind of thing it was, if it did; how it should be Named or Defined; and - according to some - whether it was done Rightly or Justly.

"Some controversies," he added, "also emerge from Interpretation of Written-Law: where either the wording is Ambiguous, or Contradictory, or appears at odds with the Spirit or Intention of the Law. And to each of these categories, there correspond specific types of Arguments and Strategies.

"There are also different Domains of Cases," Crassus said, "that must be treated distinctly from

General-Inquiries: Each has its own appropriate Topoi, or Places of Argument: some take place during Trials in Judicial Settings; others within Deliberative Settings; and a third type, Encomia, deals with Praise or Blame of particular persons. In Trials, we pursue what is Just and Equitable; in Deliberation, what is Useful and Advantageous to the Audience or the State; and in Encomia, what pertains to the Dignity and Virtue of the Person.

"And of course, the Orator's entire Power and Capacity is traditionally divided into Five Parts. First, the Orator must Discover what he will say; then, he must Arrange what has been discovered - both in Order and with the right Moment and Judgment. Then, he must Clothe and Adorn his ideas in Speech. Fourth, he must Secure them in Memory. Finally, he must Deliver them with Dignity and Charm.

"I was also taught," Crassus said, "that before even entering the core of the matter, the Speaker must begin by Winning the Goodwill of the Audience. Next, he must Present the Facts. Then, he must Establish the Point of Controversy. After that, he should Prove what he sets out to defend. Then, Refute whatever is said against him. At the end, he should Amplify and Elevate the points in his favor, and Weaken and Break Down the claims of the opposing side."

XXXII. Art was Born from Eloquence

"I had also listened," Crassus continued, "to the teachings handed down regarding the Adornment of Speech itself. These began, first, with the rule that we must speak Purely and in Proper Latin; then Clearly and Lucidly; then Ornately; and finally - with regard to the Dignity of the Subject - Fittingly, and with a kind of Inner Grace. I became familiar with the Precepts of each of these aims, one by one.

"And even in those matters that seem most tied to Natural-Endowment, I still saw that Art was brought in: for example, in the realm of Delivery and Memory, there were short but significant Precepts, to be practiced with great diligence. Indeed, nearly all the instruction of these Technical-Masters revolves around these aspects. And I would be lying," Crassus said, "if I claimed that such teachings offer no help at all. They do serve to remind the Speaker of where each element might be placed - and help ensure that, when he looks to a Target or Aim, he doesn't stray too far from what he set out to accomplish.

"Still," he went on, "I see the Power of such Precepts this way: not that Orators have attained Praise or Eloquence by following them, but that Eloquent Men, by their own spontaneous actions, have done these very things - and that others, observing them, gathered and systematized those practices into an Art. In this sense,

Eloquence did not come from Art, but rather Art was born from Eloquence.

"Even so," Crassus clarified, "as I've said before, I do not reject it. While perhaps not necessary for Speaking-Well, it is still not unworthy of being known. And some form of Practice must be undertaken - although, for you two, the race is already long since underway.

"But for those who are just entering the Stadium - those who are about to face the trials inside the Forum as if entering a battlefield - it is still possible to train ahead of time through Playful Rehearsals and Meditative Exercises."

Sulpicius broke in here: "That's the very thing we want to learn - this form of Practice itself. Still, I must say, we are also eager to hear, even briefly, your summary of the Art, even if we've encountered much of it before. But that can come later," he added. "Right now, we are asking: what do you believe about Practice itself?"

XXXIII. Write as much as possible

Crassus said: "I do, in fact, approve of the exercises you both regularly undertake when you take up some imagined Case resembling those that arise inside the Forum, and speak on it as precisely and persuasively as possible.

"But most people," he continued, "do nothing more than drill their voice - and not even skillfully. They strain their strength, agitate their tongues for speed, and find delight in a flood of words. The error lies here: they've heard that it is by Speaking that men learn to Speak. And while this is true in one way, it is equally true that those who Speak Badly make it even easier to Speak Badly again.

"For this reason, in these very Exercises, while it is useful to Speak Off-the-Cuff from time to time, it is even more useful to take time for Thought and speak Preparedly and with Precision. The essential point - and I'll say it plainly, though we almost never do it - is this: Writing as much as possible. For the Stylus," Crassus declared, "is the finest and most powerful Shaper and Teacher of Speaking - and not without reason.

"For if Careful Preparation and Deliberation can easily surpass Sudden and Unplanned Speech, then surely Persistent and Attentive Writing will surpass even that preparation. For whatever one draws from the Resources of Technique, or from the Wellspring of Insight and Practical Understanding - so long as one is focused on the Subject - those resources reveal themselves. They appear of their own accord to the searching mind, and present themselves to one's powers of Thought. All the Thoughts and Words that shine most brightly in each kind of speaking will rise to the edge of the Stylus - they must come forward, and take form.

"Moreover, the Arrangement and Formation of these words is perfected in Writing - not in poetic meter, but in the Rhythm and Cadence proper to Public-Speech.

"These are the things that stir Shouts of Praise and Awe among those who hear a great Orator. And no one will ever achieve them - no matter how intensely they practice Impromptu-Speaking - unless they have long and frequently engaged in Writing. Indeed, the person who moves from the Habit of Writing into Speaking carries with him a Power: even when Speaking without preparation, what he says will still seem like the work of a Written-Speech. And even when he does bring something written into his Speaking, the rest of the Speech will follow in a way similar in Style and Power.

"Just as a ship, once in motion, continues its course even after the rowers have paused - still driven by the momentum of its earlier force - so too in a Speech, when the written portion ends, the remainder of the Oration carries forward with that same momentum, stirred into motion by the Force and Form of the Writing itself."

XXXIV. Translating from Greek to Latin

"In my daily Exercises," said Crassus, "when I was a young Aristocratic-Man, I would regularly adopt a Practice I knew to be favored by our opponent, Gaius Carbo. I would select either a passage of weighty verse or a striking Oration - something I could commit to Memory

- and then, without looking at the original, I would express the same content using my own words, aiming to replicate the Meaning as closely as possible.

"But I later came to recognize a flaw in this Method: the most Precise, most Beautiful, and most Appropriate words had already been chosen - by Ennius, if I were imitating verse, or by Gracchus, if I had chosen one of his Orations. So if I reused the same words, I learned nothing; and if I chose others, I risked training myself to prefer words less fitting and less effective.

"After that, I turned to a better exercise - and as a youth, I committed myself to this: I would take the Orations of the greatest Greek Speakers and translate them into Latin. In doing so, I gained a twofold benefit: first, I would use excellent Latin words that were nonetheless familiar; and second, I found myself forging new expressions by imitation - words that were new to our own language but still entirely apt.

"As for Voice, Breath, Bodily-Movement, and even the Gestures of the Tongue - these things require not so much Technical-Art as Labor, Diligence, and Careful-Selection of Models. In all such things, it is most important to identify to whom we give close attention, to whom we imitate, and to whom we wish to resemble. Let us look not only to Orators, but even to Stage-Actors - so that we do not, through bad habits, fall into deformities or uncouth mannerisms."

"Memory, too, must be exercised: commit to heart as many passages as possible, whether from our own writings or from others. I myself do not disapprove of that Method - if you've learned it - of employing Images and Memory-Spaces, the one taught in certain Schools of Technique."

"But from there," he went on, "this household Practice-Ground, this Shadow-Exercise, must be brought out into the fray - into the middle of the crowd, the dust, the shouting, the battlefield inside the Forum. Within that space, one must undergo the use of every skill and test the strength of one's Mind. What was once practiced in the Darkness of Rehearsal must be brought into the Light of Truth.

"One must also read the Poets, learn the Histories, read and re-read all the Authors and Teachers of the Liberal-Arts. And, for the sake of practice, one should Praise, Interpret, Revise, Criticize, and Refute. One should argue both sides of every Question, and whatever seems Persuasive in any matter should be Drawn-Out and Spoken-Aloud.

"One must thoroughly learn everything there is about Res Publica - the Civil Law, study the Statutes, absorb all Ancient Traditions, the customs of the Senate, the structure of the Republic, the Rights of our Allies, the Treaties, the Bonds, and the Causes of Empire itself.

"And finally," Crassus added, "one must sip from every kind of Urban-Wit - a certain Playfulness and Charm, like a sprinkling of salt, with which the entire Speech is to be seasoned.

"I have poured out to you everything I believe," he concluded. "And perhaps, had you pulled aside any ordinary household Aristocratic-Man from some circle of conversation away from animal laborens, he too would have offered you the same answers, had you pressed him with the same questions."

XXXV. Pleas for Crassus to Continue

When Crassus had spoken these words, a silence followed. Yet although it seemed to all present that he had said enough for the matter at hand, they nevertheless felt that his conclusion had arrived far more swiftly than they would have wished.

Then Scaevola said: "What's the matter, Cotta? Why the silence? Has nothing come to mind that you'd like to ask Crassus further?"

"On the contrary, by Hercules!" replied Cotta, "I was paying close attention. For the rush of his words was so great, and the Oration flew so swiftly, that while I grasped its Force and Momentum, I could scarcely Perceive its Entrance or Path.

"It was as if I had stepped into some lavish and overflowing house - not with its tapestries unfurled, or its silver laid out, or its paintings and statues on open display - but with all these splendid and magnificent things heaped together and veiled.

"In just the same way, in Crassus' Oration I caught sight of the Wealth and Ornaments of his Intellect, but only through certain veils and wrappings. And though I longed to gaze upon them clearly, I was hardly given the chance. I cannot say, then, that I am completely unaware of what he possesses - yet neither can I say I Truly-Know or Have-Seen."

Scaevola rejoined: "Well, then, why don't you do just what you would in that house full of treasures? If everything were tucked away, as you say, and you were full of eager curiosity, wouldn't you ask, especially if you were on friendly terms with him, the Master of the House to have ***it brought (******the slaves bring it***) out for display? Then do the same now: ask Crassus to bring into the Light that Great-Abundance of Oratorical Ornaments (***Harmonious-Words***), which, though built into a Single-Structure, we have only glimpsed in passing - as though through a window-lattice."

"I do ask," said Cotta, "but I ask through you, Scaevola - for both I and Sulpicius are restrained by a certain modesty before the most dignified of men. Crassus, after all, has always held in contempt this sort of discussion. These inquiries may seem mere childish elements to him. But you, Scaevola, please grant us this request. Persuade Crassus to unfold and expand for us those things he so tightly compressed and narrowly confined in his speech."

"By Hercules!" said Mucius, "Before now I desired this more for your sake than for mine. For I do not long so much for Crassus' discussion of these things as I delight in his Orations when he Speaks in real cases. But now, Crassus, I too ask - on my own behalf - that since we have as much Leisure-with-Dignity as we've had in a long time, you not hesitate to construct the full edifice of what you have begun. The shape of this whole undertaking appears to me greater and finer than I had imagined - and I wholeheartedly approve of it."

XXXVI. Civil Law 'Orators'

Then Crassus said: "Truly, Scaevola, I cannot help but marvel that even you desire these things? Things which I myself do not possess in the manner of those who teach them, nor are they of the sort that - even if I did master them perfectly - would be worthy of your Wisdom or of your ears."

"What's this?" Scaevola replied. "If you believe that even those ordinary and well-circulated doctrines are scarcely fit to be heard by this young age - do you then think we may also neglect those matters which you yourself said the Orator must come to understand? I mean: the Natures of Human-Beings, the Mores of the

Citizens, the Principles by which the Minds of Men are stirred or restrained, the Knowledge of History, of Antiquity, of the Management of the Res Publica, and finally - even our own Civil Law? For I always believed that all such Knowledge - this entire Abundance of Things - was contained in your Practical-Wisdom. But I had never seen such a rich storehouse as part of the equipment of an Orator."

Then Crassus said: "Well then - to leave aside countless other matters, vast and innumerable, and to come directly to your own Civil Law - those men whom you waited for through many hours, while in a hurry to reach the Campus Martius - do you consider them to be Orators?"

At this, Crassus laughed.

Scaevola groaned: "You mean when Hypsaeus - in a loud voice and with a flood of words - petitioned the praetor Marcus Crassus, begging that the man he was defending be allowed to lose his case? And when Gnaeus Octavius - a man of consular rank - gave a no less long-winded speech, insisting that his adversary not lose his case, so that the man for whom he was speaking might not be freed, through the folly of the opposing side, from a shameful charge of mismanagement and from all further trouble?"

Crassus continued: "Well I, for one, remember Mucius once told me the story - would not consider those men worthy of the name Orator - in fact, not even worthy of the inside of the Forum.

"But still," said Crassus, "those advocates did not lack Eloquence, nor Method in Speaking, nor Verbal Abundance - but what they lacked was Prudence in Civil Law. For one of them, by his legal motion, demanded more than what the Law of the Twelve Tables permitted - and so, though he succeeded in his request, the case was lost. The other believed it unjust that the case against him should go beyond the terms of the Action - but he failed to understand Civil Law with Prudence because if such an Action had been accepted, his adversary would have lost the entire suit."

XXXVII. Civil Law: Shame and Eloquence

"What then?" Crassus continued. "Just a few days ago - were we not seated together on the tribunal of our friend, Quintus Pompeius, the Urban Praetor - when a man, counted among the so-called 'Skilled-in-Speaking,' demanded that a Standard and Well-Worn Exception be granted to the Defendant: namely, 'That the due-date of the money had not yet come'?

"He failed entirely to understand that this Exception exists for the sake of the Plaintiff - to protect him if the Defendant could prove, to the judge, that the money had been demanded before it was actually owed. For in that case, the Plaintiff - seeking again to recover the same money - would not be barred by the Exception, since the matter had previously been brought to trial.

"What, then, could be more Disgraceful - or more Laughable - than this: that a man who has taken up the Role of defending the disputes and Causes of his friends, who is expected to assist the burdened, to heal the distressed, to lift up the fallen - should stumble so badly over the smallest and most trivial of matters, that some look on him with pity, and others with ridicule?

"For my part," Crassus continued, "I think our kinsman, Publius Crassus - that Crassus the Rich - ought to be especially praised. Though he was a refined and accomplished man in many things, I think he deserves the highest admiration for this: that, though his own brother was Publius Scaevola, he still frequently told him that he could not rightly fulfill the demands of Civil Law - unless he also acquired the Abundance of Speaking. This is something his son - the very man who was consul with me - indeed achieved.

"And what of Marcus Cato? Was he not a man of such Eloquence as that age and that Republic could bear at its fullest? And was he not also the most expert in Civil Law of them all?

"I speak of these things with some hesitation, out of modesty," Crassus added, "since present here is a man of the highest rank in Speaking - the one Orator I admire above all others. But even he - as you know well - has always scorned Civil Law.

"Still," he concluded, "since you have wished to share in my view and judgment on these matters, I will hide nothing from you. And as long as I am able, I will lay before you what I truly believe about each concern."

XXXVIII. Impudent Ignorance in Small Vessels

"Antonius," Crassus said, "truly possesses an astonishing, nearly singular, and even Divine-Force of Genius. And although he has been left bare of this Particular-Knowledge of Civil Law, he still seems able to defend himself by other arms of Practical-Wisdom. So let us set him aside from what I now say.

"But for the rest, I will not hesitate: first, I Judge them guilty of inertia - a kind of willful idleness; and then, of shamelessness. For what could be more shameless than this: to wander about inside the Forum, to attach oneself constantly to the Laws and the tribunals of the Praetors, to handle Private Trials concerning matters of the utmost gravity - where the dispute is often not over fact, but over Equity and the structure of Right - to throw oneself into Causes before the Centumviral Court, where all the most intricate elements of Law are examined:

-Laws of Usucapion and Guardianship,

-Laws of Kinship and Agnation,

-Questions of Accretion and Overflow,

-Issues of Bondage,

-Property Transfers,

-Rights over Walls, Light, and Water Flow,

-Wills confirmed or annulled

-and countless others;

and yet to have no idea what is one's own and what is another's, or - at the most basic level - what makes a person a Citizen or a Foreigner, a Slave or a Free Man?

"This is impudent ignorance, of the most flagrant kind. Even worse is the laughable arrogance of those who confess they are unskilled in the smaller vessels, but then boast they are trained to steer the quinquereme - or even something larger!

"You mean to say," Crassus continued, "that you are deceived in court by a single clause of your opponent's contract - and when you seal the tablets of your own client, you trap him in writing he cannot escape - and still I am supposed to entrust you with any Major-Cause?

"By Hercules! I would sooner entrust the Argo itself to a man who capsized a rowboat in the harbor, than assign you a Great-Cause before the People! And what if the Causes are not Small at all - but the Greatest - precisely those in which the Civil Law is most in question? What face must that patron wear, who dares to approach such matters without any Knowledge of Law?

"What Cause could be Greater than the one of the soldier whose death had been falsely reported by a messenger from the army, and whose father, believing the news, altered his will and appointed another heir. The father then died. But the soldier returned alive, and brought suit to claim his paternal inheritance, having been disinherited not by name, but by silence.

"Now in this case, which came before the Centumviral Court, the question turned entirely on the Principles of Civil Law: Could a son be disinherited from his father's estate if the will neither named him heir nor explicitly excluded him?

"That," Crassus concluded, "is the kind of Case one must be prepared to speak on - and no Orator should ever claim authority in such matters who has not been shaped by the Inner-Structure of Civil Law."

XXXIX. Four Causes

"And what of that Great-Cause," Crassus continued, "which was judged between the noble houses of the Marcelli and the patrician Claudii before the Centumviral Court - when the Marcelli claimed inheritance through the bloodline of a freedman's son, and the Claudii argued that, by Gentile-Right, the estate had reverted to them? In that Cause, was it not necessary for the Orators to speak from within the Full-Depth of the Law of Lineage and Gentile-Kinship?

"And again: there was a Cause, also judged before the Centumviri, in which the question arose whether a man who had come to Rome in exile - and who, according to law, was permitted to remain there in banishment - could, by attaching himself to someone as if he were his Patron, be said to belong to his household. He had died intestate. And was it not in that trial that the obscure and little-known Right of Application was brought to light - explained and clarified by his Advocate?

"Consider, too, a more Recent-Cause - one in which I myself defended Caius Sergius Orata in a Private Trial, with our Antonius here speaking for the opposing side. Was not our entire defense conducted from within the Law? For when Marius Gratidianus had sold a house to Orata, and failed to declare in the legal formula of the sale that a portion of the building was subject to an easement, we argued that - if any defect or burden had existed and the seller had known of it yet failed to disclose it - then he was bound to compensate.

"In such cases, even our friend Marcus Bucculeius - a man not, in my judgment, foolish, and in his own opinion quite wise, and not without affection for the Study of Law - recently erred in a very similar matter. For when he sold a house to Lucius Fufius, he included in the sale the provision: 'the lights (windows) shall remain as they now are.' But Fufius, as soon as construction began in some distant part of the city - in a place that only barely could be seen from the windows of the house - brought suit against Bucculeius, claiming that any obstruction of any portion of the sky, however remote, would constitute a violation of the agreement regarding light.

"And what of that most Celebrated-Cause of Manius Curius and Marcus Coponius - argued recently before the Centumviri, in a court packed with people, awaited with intense anticipation? In that case, our contemporary and colleague Quintus Scaevola - a man most thoroughly trained in the discipline of Civil Law, and sharpened by both natural insight and practiced judgment, polished and subtle in speech - defended the laws of testaments, relying on written formulas. He argued that unless a Posthumous Heir was both born and then died before falling under the legal guardianship of the testator, one could not become heir in his place - even if named in the will as heir after such a Posthumous.

"I, on the other hand, defended the intention of the man who made the testament - that if there was no son to come into guardianship, then Manius Curius was to be the rightful heir.

"Now, did either of us in this great trial ever depart from Authority, from Examples, or from the Formulas of Wills? Did we not both move and speak from the very center of Civil Law?

XL. The Greatest Cause of Civil Law

"But I set aside the countless other examples of Vast-Causes, for they are truly innumerable. Yet I must emphasize this: even our very lives may come to turn upon the intricacies of Civil Law.

"Take the case of Gaius Mancinus, that most noble and honorable man, a former Consul. After the disgrace of the Numantine Treaty, the Fetial Priest, following a Senate Decree, formally surrendered him to the Numantines. But they refused to accept him. Later, Mancinus returned to Rome and, thinking nothing of it, entered inside the Senate as usual. At once, Publius Rutilius, son of Marcus and Tribune of the Plebs, ordered him to be led outside of the Senate - claiming that Mancinus was no longer a Citizen. For it had been handed down in tradition that anyone surrendered by either the Father (pater familias), the Roman People, or the Fetial Priest - whether by sale or treaty - forfeited postliminium and could not re-enter the Civic Body.

"Now, what Greater-Cause can we imagine among all matters of the Civitas than one concerning a man's Political Rank, Citizenship, Freedom, and even his Personhood? And what makes this all the more serious is that the case turned not upon a criminal charge that could be denied - but entirely upon Civil Law.

"In a similar kind of case - though of lower social rank - imagine someone from a Federated-People who had served in Rome as a Slave, had then been freed, and later returned to his homeland. Our ancestors debated whether such a man had, through postliminium, returned to his original people, or whether he had lost Roman Citizenship.

"Or take the question of Freedom itself - about which there is no more serious Judgment. Must there not also be Legal Contention when it is asked whether someone who was registered in the census with the will of his master became free immediately, or only after the lustrum was completed?

"Consider also the famous case, preserved in the Memory of our fathers: a Roman paterfamilias returned from Spain, having left behind a pregnant wife in the province. In Rome, without sending a formal notice of divorce, he married another woman. He then died intestate. From each woman, a son was born. A dispute arose - surely not a small matter! - about which of the two sons was legitimate, and whether the second woman was a wife or merely a concubine. For the Judgment turned on a legal phrase: whether, through subsequent marriage alone, a divorce from the first had occurred.

"Now then - if someone ignorant of the Civil Law dares to walk about inside the Forum tall and upright, lively in expression and bright of countenance, darting his eyes this way and that, followed by a great train of dependents, offering his advice as a protection to clients and a resource to friends - indeed, presenting himself as a Llight to nearly all Citizens in their times of need - should we not consider it among the greatest disgraces?"

XLI. Crassus Offers a Prelude

Crassus continued: "And since I have already spoken of shamelessness, let me now also chastise the laziness and inertia of certain men. For even if the knowledge of Civil Law were vast and difficult, the sheer magnitude of its usefulness ought to compel men to undertake the labor of learning it.

"But, O Immortal Gods! - and I would not say this in the presence of Scaevola, unless he himself often said it - I know no art whose mastery seems easier to him than this one. And yet many think otherwise, for particular reasons. First, those Ancients who once held mastery in this Domain - out of a desire to preserve and expand their own Power - refused to make their Art Public. Then later, once it had been made Public - when Gnaeus Flavius was the first to publish the formulas of Legal Actions - no one followed to arrange and order these matters according to their Inner-Logic and by Proper-Categories.

"But there is nothing, truly, that can be made into an Art unless the person attempting it already possesses a firm grasp of the things from which that Art would arise.

For only someone with True-Knowledge of those things can transform them into an ordered Art - even when that Art has not yet been formally devised.

"Now, I see that - trying to be brief - I may have expressed this somewhat obscurely. But let me try again, and say it, if I can, more clearly."

XLII. The Ultimate End of Civil Law

Crassus continued: "Nearly everything that is now contained within an Art was once scattered and fragmented. In the case of Music, there were once only numbers, tones, and modes, without any Formal-Union. In Geometry, one found lines, shapes, intervals, and magnitudes - but not yet Bound-Together into a single coherent system. In Astrology, there were merely the revolutions of the heavens, the risings, settings, and motions of stars, Un-Bound by law or theory.

"In Grammar, there existed the interpretation of poets, knowledge of histories, translation of words, and a certain musicality of articulation. Even in this very Domain of Speaking - with its Five Operations: Invention, Ornamentation, Arrangement, Memory, and Delivery - each part once drifted apart, unknown to all and widely diffused.

"Then, a kind of Art from a different kind of Domain altogether, one claimed in its entirety by the Philosopher-Men was applied from outside. This Bound-

Together what had been dispersed and torn apart, and, with a kind of internal Reasoning-Bond held the Domain together.

"Let us then declare that the ultimate End of Civil Law is this: the preservation of lawful and customary equity among citizens in both things and causes.

"Next, one must discern the Kinds of Civil Law involved, and reduce their multitude to a fixed number and limited structure. A Kind is that which contains Parts that differ in Appearance, yet share a common Underlying-Form. And Parts are those Sub-Elements which are contained within the Kinds from which they emerge.

"All such Kinds and Parts - whenever named - must be accompanied by Definitions, which express what Power or Force belongs to the thing named. For a Definition is a concise and circumscribed account of the proper elements belonging to the thing we seek to define.

"I would offer examples of these things," Crassus said, "were it not plain to me who is present for this dialogue. So instead, I will briefly gather the point I proposed.

"If I myself were permitted to carry out what I've long been contemplating - or if someone else should take it up, either while I am hindered or after I am gone - and were he to organize all of Civil Law into its few Principal-Kinds, then divide these into their respective Branches, then declare the unique Force of each one through clear Definitions - you would at last possess a perfect Art of Civil Law. And this Art would be rich and expansive, rather than difficult and obscure.

"But even now, while all these things remain unbound and dispersed, one may still gather and collect them from every side, and be filled with a sufficient and complete Knowledge of Civil Law."

XLIII. The Twelve Tables (Living Ancients)

"Do you not see," Crassus continued, "that even a Roman Knight - Gaius Aculeo, the man I have long lived beside, and who still lives beside me - though he is a man of the sharpest mind and least trained in the other Arts, still grasps Civil Law so well that, when you leave this place, none among even the most learned can rightly be placed before him?

"For everything in Civil Law lies before one's eyes, embedded in daily use, in the intercourse of citizens, and in the Forum itself. Nor is it buried in many Letters or vast volumes. For these same matters have first been brought forth by many, and then - by altering only a few words - have been written down repeatedly, even by the same authors.

"Moreover," he added, "there is something most astonishing here - though many do not recognize it. The easiness with which Civil Law may be grasped and learned is joined to a kind of delight and sweetness in the act of knowing it. If a person is charmed by Aelian studies - that is, by Antiquarian investigation - there is no greater treasury than Civil Law: in the Law itself, in the books of the Pontiffs, and especially in the Twelve Tables, one finds a living Image of Antiquity. For not only does the ancient form of words shine forth, but also the modes of action and customary ways of life of our Ancestors are revealed.

"If one instead contemplates Civil Knowledge as such - what Scaevola, to be sure, does not think belongs to the Orator proper, but to some other species of Prudence - still, one would see that all of it is contained within the Twelve Tables, where the benefits and parts of our entire Civil Community are written out in order.

"And even if someone finds joy in that exalted and glorious thing called Philosophy, then - let me speak boldly - he will find the wellsprings of all his discourse flowing out of Civil Law and Legislation. For from this Law we see what is most worth seeking: that the True, Just, and Honorable-Labor is adorned with Honors, Rewards, and Glory, while the Vices and Frauds of men are struck with Penalties, Disgrace, Bonds, Beatings, Banishment, and Death.

"And through this, we are taught - not by endless, tangled disputes - but by the Authority and Nod of the Laws themselves: to tame our desires, to restrain every impulse, to guard what is ours, and to keep our minds, eyes, and hands away from what belongs to others."

XLIV. Twelve Tables Surpasses All of Philosophy

Crassus continued: "Let them all shout if they wish - I will still speak my mind. By Hercules, I declare this: the single little book of the Twelve Tables, if one has truly seen the Sources and Heads of Law, seems to me to surpass the entire libraries of all the Philosophers - both in the weight of its Authority and the richness of its Usefulness.

"And if there is anything that ought to delight us above all else, it is our Native Land. The force and nature of that Love are so strong that even the Wisest Man - as the tale goes - preferred that craggy Ithaca, fixed like a nest upon the roughest of rocks, to immortality itself.

"How much more, then, should we be inflamed by love for this Homeland, which alone among all the lands of the earth is the House of Virtue, of Dominion, of Dignity! And the Mind, the Custom, the Discipline of that Homeland must be known to us - either because she is our Motherland, the Parent of us all, or because such Wisdom must have existed in the making of her Civil Law as existed in the conquest and gathering of her Great Empire.

"You will also experience from the study of Civil Law a kind of joy and delight, which comes from this: you will far more easily perceive how greatly our Ancestors surpassed all other peoples in Prudence, if you compare our Laws with those of Lycurgus, Draco, or Solon. For it is almost beyond belief how formless - and nearly laughable - all Civil Law seems to be, outside of our own Roman system. I have often said this in daily conversation, when comparing the Prudence of our own men with that of others - and especially with the Greeks.

"For all these reasons, Scaevola, I said that for those who wish to become Perfect Orators, the Knowledge of Civil Law is absolutely necessary."

XLV. Honor of Being Part of Civil Law

Cassus continued: "And indeed, who is unaware of how much Honor, Gratitude, and Dignity is brought to those who preside over Civil Law, simply by the very nature of that Knowledge? Thus it is not as among the Greeks, where the lowest of men, drawn in by some little fee, offer themselves as servants to the Orators in trials - those whom they call pragmatikoi.

By contrast, in our Republic, it is the most distinguished and illustrious men who take up this role - like that man, whom the greatest of our Poets praised precisely for his Civil Law expertise, calling him: "A man deeply wise in heart: sagacious Sextus Aelius." And many others besides, who - though their native Intelligence earned them dignity - have gone further and completed their excellence in such a way that, through their answers in Law, their Authority carried even more weight than their Intellect alone.

Now what refuge could be more honorable for old age - more suited to be celebrated and adorned - than the Interpretation of Law? As for me, I secured this support already in my youth, not only for use in Forum Causes, but as an adornment and honor for my old age - so that when my powers begin to fail (as that time is now fast approaching), I may free my home from solitude through these Civil Law pursuits.

"What could be more noble than for an elder, who has fulfilled the duties of office and Republic, to rightly declare the same thing that Apollo the Pythian proclaims in Ennius: 'I am he from whom, if not 'kings and peoples', then at least all citizens - Unsure of their affairs - seek counsel; Whom I render certain from uncertainty, who leave with plans made firm, so they do not recklessly disturb chaotic things.'

"For the House of the Jurist is, without a doubt, the Oracle of the Whole Republic. Let the doorway and the vestibule of this very Q. Mucius stand as witness: even in his feeble health and advanced age, his home is still daily crowded by the greatest citizens - adorned with the splendor of noble men.

XLVI. Crassus Stretches a Finger to Public Law (Not A Long Argument)

Crassus continued: "Why I believe that Public Laws, too, the ones belonging properly to the Civic Body and the Republic's Power, along with Records of Deeds and Examples from Antiquity, ought to be familiar to the Orator - this scarcely requires a long argument.

"For just as, in private cases and legal trials, the Orator must often summon his speech from the Civil Law, and thus - as we have already said - the Knowledge of Civil Law is necessary to the Orator, so too in Public Cases - in trials, in Assemblies, in the Senate - it is the whole Memory of Antiquity, the Authority of Public Law, and the Rational-Science of Directing the Republic that ought to serve as his material, provided to those Orators who move within the affairs of the Res Publica.

"Our Inquiry doesn't seek out just some Legal-Advocate, nor a Town-Crier, nor some Shouting-Rhetorician - but rather the sort of Aristocratic-Man who, first of all, stands as High-Priest of that Art of the Orator, which - even though Nature herself had given man a great Native-Capacity for it - was still believed to be bestowed by the gods. So much so, indeed, that Public-Speech itself - though proper to Man - was not thought to have been discovered by us, but Divinely-Delivered.

"Next, clothed in the name of Orator, he should be the one bearing the Staff of Hermes upright - even amidst the weapons of enemies.

"Then too, the Orator must be one who, through Speech, can subject the Crimes and Deceits of the Guilty to the Hatred of Citizens and bind them to Punishment - and likewise, with the Shield of Intelligence, liberate the Innocent from the penalties of Judgment.

"He should also have the Power to rouse a languishing and faltering People to Honor, or to lead them away from Error, or to inflame them against the Wicked, or, when they are aroused against the Good, to temper their wrath. Finally, whatever emotional motion the situation or the Cause stirs up in the minds of men, the Orator must be able either to arouse it or to soothe it with Speech.

"If anyone thinks that this Power has already been fully laid out by those who have written on the Method of Speaking, or that I could explain it now in such a short time - he is sorely mistaken. He fails to perceive not only my own lack of expertise, but also the magnitude of the subject itself. For my part - since you have asked for it - I believed I ought only to point out the Fountains from which you might drink, and to indicate the Paths themselves - not to act as your guide, for that would be both endless and unnecessary, but rather, as is customary, merely to stretch out my finger and gesture toward the Sources."

XLVII. Mucius Compares Crassus to Socrates

"Well then," said Mucius, "it seems to me, Crassus, that you have more than fulfilled your duty to those young Aristocratic-Men in their pursuits - if, indeed, they are truly earnest in them. For just as they say of Socrates, that he believed his task complete whenever someone had been stirred, by his encouragement alone, toward the pursuit and grasp of Virtue - and that once a man was convinced that there was nothing he'd rather be than Good, then all the rest of Learning would follow easily - so too do I now understand this: if these young Men are willing to enter into the things that Crassus has opened up through his Speech, then the doorway having been flung open, they will find the path to what they desire most a very smooth ascent."

"Indeed," said Sulpicius, "to us this has been both most welcome and deeply delightful. Yet still, there are a few things we would ask - especially this: you, Crassus, passed rather swiftly over the very Art itself, even as you confessed both that you did not despise it and that you had studied it. If you were to elaborate on that a little more fully, you would entirely satisfy our long-standing desire. For now we have understood what things ought to be studied - and that alone is a great benefit - but we also long to know the Paths, and the Method, that lead to those things."

"Well then," said Crassus, "since I - for the sake of keeping you here with me - have followed your wishes rather than my own Custom or Nature, shall we perhaps call upon Antonius? Let us ask him to unfold those things which he has long kept within, the very things from which, as he once complained, 'a whole little book accidentally escaped' - and so, let him now reveal to us those Mysteries of Speaking."

"As you see fit," said Sulpicius. "For when Antonius speaks, we will also come to understand what you, Crassus, mean."

"Then I ask you, Antonius," said Crassus, "since it is now laid upon us by these young men and their studies, that we bear the burden, I ask that you unfold for them what you understand concerning these matters - matters which, as you can plainly see, they now seek from you."

XLVIII. Antonius and His Little Book

"I plainly see," said Antonius, "that I have been caught - and I feel it, too. Not only because these young men now demand from me the sort of things I neither know nor cultivate, but because - what I always avoid in courtroom Causes - I now cannot escape following you, Crassus. They will not allow me to.

"Still, I will step more boldly into what you all desire - especially because I expect I shall have the same advantage here in this Dialogue as I do in actual Public-Speaking: namely, that no one will expect a highly adorned or stylized Speech. For I will not be speaking about an Art - which I have never learned - but rather about my own Habit. And those things which I once collected into my little notebook were not derived from any formal Doctrine passed down to me, but were forged in the very midst of Practice and Real Causes. If these reflections do not meet your approval, you must not blame me, but your own unfairness - for asking such things from someone who openly admits he does not know them. Praise rather my willingness, since I have responded not from my own judgment but because of your eagerness, and have done so without reluctance."

"Go on then," said Crassus, "for there is no risk that anything you say will be unwise - such that any one of us might regret having urged you into this Speech."

"I will go on, then," said Antonius. "And I will begin with what I consider necessary in all such Disputations: namely, that we must first clarify the very thing under discussion. Otherwise, the Speech may wander and go astray - especially if the speakers, while disagreeing, have not even agreed on what the matter itself is.

"For example: if the question were 'What is the Art of the General?' - I would begin by defining the General himself. Once defined as the Administrator of War, we could then proceed to matters like the formation of Armies, the organization of Camps and Marching Orders, the alignment of Standards, the Siege of Cities, the supply lines, the laying and evading of Ambushes, and all the other elements proper to the Art of Waging War. And whoever had both the capacity and knowledge of such matters, I would call a True General - and I would bring forward the examples of Africanus and Maximus, or Epaminondas and Hannibal, and others of that kind.

"Likewise, if we were asking if one who guides the Res Publica should be called a Statesman, I would define him as the person who grasps those matters by which the well-being of the Republic is secured and increased, and who knows how to use them. That person I would call the Pilot of the Republic, the Author of Civic Counsel. And I would name Publius Lentulus, that noble figure, and Tiberius Gracchus the elder, and Quintus Metellus, Publius Africanus, and Gaius Laelius, and many others - some from our own city, others from the rest of the world.

"Or again: if the question were, 'Who is rightly called a Jurist?' - I would say: it is the one who is skilled in the Laws and in the customs by which private persons live within the city, and who can give sound counsel for replying, acting, and taking precaution. And from that category, I would name Sextus Aelius, Manius Manilius, and Publius Mucius."

XLIX. Antonius Defines the Orator

Antonius continued: "Let me now descend, if you will, to the lighter pursuits among the Disciplines. If one were to ask what makes a Musician, a Grammarian, or a Poet, I could just as clearly explain what each one professes and where, beyond their proper bounds, we should not place our demands. Even the Philosopher - that man who seems to claim mastery of all knowledge and wisdom - has his proper description: namely, the one who seeks to know the powers, natures, and causes of all things divine and human, and who pursues and grasps the full Order of Right Living. It is this man, by that task, who deserves the name Philosopher.

"But now - as we have been asking about the Orator - I must confess that I do not define him in the same expansive way as Crassus. For he appeared to me to fold the entire scope of all human knowledge and all Disciplines into a single role and title - the Orator. By contrast, I hold that the Orator is the one who can speak in a Pleasing-Manner to the ears and Persuasive to the Judgment - and who does so in Public-Causes and Civic Shared-Matters. This, for me, is the Orator: one who is additionally well-equipped with voice, gesture, and a certain graceful charm.

"Our friend Crassus, however, seemed to me to define the Orator not by the limits of an Art, but by the immeasurable boundaries of his own Genius. For he handed over, with full authority, the very rudder of the Republic into the Orator's hands - and that truly astonished me, Scaevola, that you conceded so much to him. For you yourself, with your restrained and polished brevity, have so often won the assent of the Senate on matters of the highest consequence.

"As for Marcus Scaurus, who I hear is presently in the countryside not far from here - a man supremely skilled in the Governance of the Republic - if he were to hear, Crassus, that you are claiming for the Orator the full weight of Gravitas and Counsel, I imagine he would soon arrive and - by his very gaze and presence - silence our loquacious gathering. For while he is certainly not without power in Speech, his strength lies far more in Wisdom over Great-Affairs than in the Art of Speaking.

"Nor, indeed, does the fact that someone possesses both these powers mean that one necessarily arises from the other. The man who is a Counselor of the Republic, and a Good Senator, is not for that reason an Orator. Nor is the one who is Eloquent and Persuasive in Speech, and also happens to excel in Governance, thereby showing that his mastery of Statecraft arose from his command of Speech. These Capacities are, in fact, quite distinct - far removed from one another, divergent and disjoined in path and method. Consider Marcus Cato, Publius Africanus, Quintus Metellus, Gaius Laelius - all of whom were, to be sure, eloquent men - but who adorned their Speech not by the Art of Oratory, but by the Dignity of the Republic."

L. Antonius and The Good and The Skilled Orator

Antonius continued: "There is no prohibition - neither from Nature herself, nor from any Law or Custom - that forbids a single Human-Being from possessing knowledge of more than a single Discipline. But that does not mean that, simply because Pericles of Athens was both supremely Eloquent and for many years the Principal Counselor of that city's Republic, the two Capacities must therefore be one and the same - either in the man or in the art. Nor, because Publius Crassus was both eloquent in speech and skilled in Civil Law, must we conclude that the Science of Law is somehow included within the Art of Speaking.

"For if any person, though excellent in one Art or Faculty, takes up another, and becomes skilled in both, it does not follow that this second Expertise becomes a Part of the first. By that logic, we might as well claim that ball-play and Twelve-Line Board Games belong properly to Civil Law, since Publius Mucius was adept in both. Or that Poetry and Natural Philosophy must be united, since Empedocles - a great Physicist - also composed a fine poem. And yet, even the Philosophers - who love to claim everything as their own - do not dare assert that

Geometry or Music belong properly to Philosophy, even though all admit that Plato excelled in both.

So then, if we must tolerate this desire to subsume all Disciplines into the Domain of the Orator, let us at least say this: that since Speech-Craft should not be barren and stripped bare - but adorned, rather, with a delightful and varied texture drawn from many Domains - the Good Orator ought to have heard many things, seen many things, reflected upon many matters with his own Thought, and passed through many more by way of Reading. Yet he is not to possess these matters as his own, but rather to have tasted them, as one might sample things that belong to others.

"For I do concede this much: that the Skilled Orator should not be a novice, or a greenhorn, in any field relevant to the civic world; he must not be a Foreigner or Stranger when engaged in Public Action - but rather someone seasoned, familiar, and shrewd in all those matters that concern the life inside of the Forum."

LI. Antonius Continues (Nature and Experience)

Antonius continued: "And no, Crassus, I am not at all disquieted by those Grand Tragic-Declarations you borrow - those that the Philosopher-Men love most to invoke - when you said that no one could possibly inflame the Minds of listeners by speech, or extinguish them once inflamed, unless he had fully perceived the nature of all things, along with the character and Reasoning-Capacities of Human-Beings. You concluded that Philosophy is therefore something the Orator must necessarily acquire - a claim that has compelled even the most gifted and leisured of men to expend entire lifetimes in pursuit of it.

"Now let me be clear: I do not disparage the immense wealth and majesty of that knowledge or the Art surrounding it - far from it, I admire it deeply. But for those of us who walk inside the Forum and speak before citizens, plebs, and women, it is enough to know and say only those things about Human-Character that do not violate the character of actual Human-Beings.

"For tell me - what Great and Weighty Orator, seeking to stir a Judge to anger against his adversary, ever hesitated in his speech because he didn't know what Anger was - whether it is a blazing heat of the soul, or a desire to avenge pain? And what Orator, aiming to agitate or unsettle the hearts of his audience - whether Judges or the People - ever reached for the abstract definitions uttered by the Philosopher-Men? Some of them claim that no motions of the soul ought to exist at all - and that anyone who stirs the feelings of a Judge commits a kind of unholy crime. Others - more lenient and closer to life - admit the presence of emotions, but think they should remain mild and measured, so as not to depart from a temperate account of things.

"But the Orator - he takes all these Common-Life things that are seen as harmful, grievous, or to be avoided, and he magnifies them with his words. Likewise, all that seems to be desirable or blessed by popular judgment, he adorns and amplifies. He does not wish to appear like a solitary wise man among a crowd of fools - lest the audience either mock him as an affected Greekling, or (worse) revere his brilliance and yet resent their own ignorance.

"No - he traverses the souls of men, touches their senses and minds with his words, and needs none of the elaborate classifications of the philosophers. He does not investigate whether the Highest Good resides in the Mind or in the Body, or whether it is defined by Virtue or Pleasure, or whether, as some think, these things may coexist and be linked together. Nor does he wander off into the terrain of those who claim that nothing is certain, and that no truth can be grasped or known.

"Yes - this is a vast and many-branched Discipline, full of rich and various arguments. But, Crassus, that is not what we are after. We are seeking something else, something far different. We need a man sharp of mind, trained by both Nature and Experience, one who can skillfully investigate what his Fellow-Citizens are thinking, what they are feeling, what they believe, and what they expect. For only such a man will know how to speak so as to move their minds."

LII. Antonius: Shared-Senses and Response to Crassus' Speech

Antonius continued: "The Orator must take hold of the Inner-Veins of every kind of Human-Type: of age, of order, and of those Minds and Shared-Senses belonging to whomever he is speaking before or intends to act upon. He must taste, as it were, their very Apprehensions.

"As for the books of the Philosophers - let him reserve those for a day of Tusculan rest, a time of Leisure-with-Dignity. Let him not find himself - when the time comes to Speak on Justice or Civic-Trust - forced to borrow from Plato, who, when attempting to articulate these matters in Speech, imagined and shaped an entirely new Republic in his books. So great was the gap between what he believed must be Spoken concerning Justice and the Actual-Habits of life and the Customs of established Republics.

"But if those things - which Plato praised - had truly been accepted by the People and Cities, then who, Crassus, would ever have permitted you - most Noble Man, most Eminent Leader of the Republic - to utter in the most public Assembly of your fellow Citizens, the very words you once proclaimed?

'Rescue us from our miseries! Tear us from the jaws of those whose cruelty cannot be satisfied even by our blood. Do not permit us to serve anyone - except all of you, collectively - those whom we both can and ought to serve.'

"I will pass over the 'miseries,' for in the view of those men, no Brave-Man can even exist in such a condition. I will pass over the 'jaws,' from which you cried to be rescued - lest your blood be swallowed up by an unjust Judgment - since they deny that anything like that can ever truly befall the Wise. But what of 'to serve?' Not only yourself, but the entire Senate - whose cause you then represented - you dared to say it was permissible to Serve?

"Is it possible, Crassus - according to those same philosophical authorities, whose precepts you have so fully embraced with your Orator's-Capacity - that Virtue can be said to serve? Virtue, which is always and only Free? Which, even when the very Bodies of men are seized by arms or bound in chains, still retains its own Right, its inner Law, and the untouchable Freedom belonging to all things within its Domain?

"And then - what you added next: not only that the Senate 'could' serve the People, but even that it 'ought' to. What Philosopher could ever approve such a thing? One so soft, so languid, so enervated, so entirely devoted to bodily pleasure and pain, that he could claim the Senate should Serve the People - even though the People themselves had entrusted the Power of Self-Government, like reins, into the hands of the Senate?"

LIII. Antonius: Rutilius and Structured-Teaching

Antonius continued: "And so, Crassus, when I believed that your words had been Spoken with Divine-Power - it was Publius Rutilius Rufus, a Learned-Man devoted to Structured-Teaching, who Declared not only that those words were unfit, but that they had been Spoken in a way that was Shameful and Disgraceful.

"This same Rutilius was also accustomed to harshly condemn Servius Galba - whom he claimed to have remembered well - for having stirred the People's Mercy when Lucius Scribonius brought formal Charges against him. At that time, Marcus Cato, Galba's bitter and unrelenting adversary, had spoken fiercely and with grave Severity before the Roman People - a Speech which he himself recorded in his Origines.

"Rutilius reproached Galba for this: that in the midst of his trial brought by Lucius Scribonius, Galba had lifted up the young Quintus - the orphaned son of his own kinsman, Gaius Sulpicius Gallus - and nearly carried him on his shoulders before the Assembly, so that the People might be moved by the Memory of a Noble Father now lost. He even brought forth his own two young sons and entrusted them publicly to the Guardianship of the People - saying, as if he were a soldier drafting his final will in the field of battle, that the Roman People themselves should be appointed as their Tutor in the face of their Orphaned Future.

"And so, though Galba at that time was surrounded by Public-Outrage and Civic-Hostility, Rutilius claimed that he was freed from Punishment by these Tragedies. I see, too, that this same episode is recorded in Cato's own writings: 'Had he not used those Children and Tears, he would have suffered Penalty.'

"These actions Rutilius strongly condemned. He said that such Humbling-Theatrics - so far beneath the dignity of an Aristocratic-Man - should be answered with Exile, or even Death, rather than Submission. And this was not mere Speech - Rutilius Believed it, Lived it, and Acted upon it. For that Aristocratic-Man, as you know, was the very model of Civic-Integrity. None in the Republic was more Upright or Sacred in his Public-Life.

"And not only did he refuse to supplicate the Judges, but he would not even permit his Defense to be spoken in a manner more Ornamented or Free than the bare Simplicity that the Truth itself demanded. He granted a small part of the Defense to our Cotta here - a young man of Supreme-Eloquence and his own sister's son. Quintus Mucius also spoke briefly in that trial brought by Lucius Scribonius, in his usual fashion: without display, pure and clear in Expression.

"But had you, Crassus, spoken then - had you, who just now argued that the Orator must borrow support from those very Philosophical Disciplines - had you been permitted to speak not in the way of Philosophers, but in your own way: then even those villainous, pestilent Citizens - worthy as they were of Punishment - would have had their savagery torn from the very roots of their Souls by the force of your Public-Speech.

"Instead, that Noble-Man - Rutilius - was lost, precisely because the Cause was pleaded as if it had taken place in that imaginary Republic of Plato's invention. No one Groaned. No Advocate Cried-Out. No one Felt any Pain. No one Protested. No one Implored the Republic. No one begged for him. In short? - not a single foot struck on the floor in protest. As if, I suppose, they feared the Stoics might be informed."

LIV. Antonious Discusses Socrates

Antonious continued: "Rutilius, that Roman-Man of Consular rank - imitated none other than the ancient Socrates. And yet, when that man - judged the wisest of all, and one who had lived most sacredly - stood to speak in his own defense at a Trial for his Life, he did so not as a Supplicant or a Defendant, but rather as if he were a Master - or even a Sovereign - set above his Judges.

"Indeed, it is told that when Lysias, the most articulate Orator of his age, brought Socrates a prepared Speech - carefully composed for use in his Defense - Socrates read it without protest and admitted it was finely written. "But," he said, "just as if you had brought me a pair of Sicyonian sandals - well-fitted and finely crafted though they be - I still would not wear them, for they are not manly.

"In the same way," he continued, "this Speech of yours - however polished and Orator-like - does not appear to me strong or manly. And so, Socrates too was condemned. Not only by the First Votes - which determined guilt or acquittal - but even by the Second Votes, which, by Athenian law, allowed the Judges to impose Sentencing. For in Athens, once a man had been found guilty (so long as the penalty did not involve direct Fraud against the State), a kind of Penalty-Appraisal would follow. The convicted man was asked what he believed he most deserved as a consequence of his actions.

"And when Socrates was asked this, he replied: that he was deserving of the highest Honors and Rewards, and that he ought to receive, at Public Expense, a daily meal in the Prytaneum - the place reserved for Greece's most Honored Citizens. This response so enraged the Judges that they condemned to death a man who was, by all accounts, entirely Innocent of any real Crime.

And indeed - had he been acquitted, which, by Hercules, I would have greatly wished (even if the matter does not touch us directly), if only for the grandeur of his Mind - how could we possibly endure these Philosophers of ours today, who, even now, though Socrates was condemned for no fault other than his Ignorance of Public-Speaking, nevertheless insist that the precepts of Speaking ought to be drawn from their School?

"I do not quarrel with them over whether their approach is better or more True. I say only this: That is one thing - and this is another. And this - without that - can still reach the highest summit.

LV. Antonius: Inherited Dignity of Civil Law

Antonius continued: "As for your embrace of Civil Law, Crassus - so ardent and complete - I see clearly what your intention was. I saw it already when you first spoke. First, you devoted yourself to Scaevola, a man whom all of us rightly love for his extraordinary grace of Character. And when you observed that his Art - though profound - was bare and unadorned, you enriched it with the dowry of your Words, clothing it in Eloquence.

"Next, because you had spent so much Labor and Time upon that Study - since the very one who encouraged and instructed you in it was a Teacher in your own home - you feared that, unless you elevated this Art of Law with your Speech, all your Effort might seem wasted.

"Still, I do not contend even with that Art itself. Let it be, by all means, as great as you wish to proclaim it. Without controversy, it is vast, far-reaching, relevant to many, always held in high Honor, and even now guided by our most illustrious Citizens. But consider this, Crassus - lest, in seeking to adorn the Knowledge of Civil Law with a new and Foreign Ornament, you end up stripping it of its own rightful and inherited dignity. For if you had declared that whoever is a Jurist is thereby also an Orator, and likewise that whoever is an Orator must also be a Jurist, you would then be establishing two Noble Arts - equal in Rank, and joined in shared Honor.

"But as things stand, you admit that a Jurist may indeed exist without the Eloquence we are discussing - and that, in fact, many such men have existed. Yet you deny that anyone may be an Orator unless he has acquired that very Juridical Knowledge. So it seems that the Jurist, in your view, is nothing on his own - nothing but a kind of Cautious and Clever Law-Tinker, a Proclaimer of Legal Auctions, a Singer of Formulas, a syllable-snaring legal technician.

"And yet - because the Orator frequently needs the help of Law in arguing Causes - you have attached that Juridical Knowledge to Eloquence, as if it were some handmaid or attendant-servant, following along behind."

LVI. Antonious: The Story of Galba and Crassus

Antonius continued: "Now, as for your astonishment, Crassus, at the audacity of those Advocates who - either knowing little - dared to profess much, or who undertook to handle the most complex matters of Civil Law Causes though they had neither studied nor understood them: both charges are easily and swiftly answered. For it is hardly surprising that a man who does not know the precise formula by which a Coemptio is enacted might nevertheless competently defend the Cause of the woman who underwent that ritual. Nor, by analogy, is it any more strange that one might be capable of navigating a large ship though he never studied the language used to launch a small one. Just so, a man who does not know the formula for a summons concerning inheritance might still successfully plead a case involving the division of a family estate.

"And as for those Centumviral-Causes you listed - Cases where the Law is said to dominate entirely - what was the Cause among them that could not, with greatest Ornament, have been argued by an Eloquent-Man untrained in Law? Even in those very Causes - such as the one concerning Marcus Curius, which you yourself recently argued; or that of Gaius Hostilius Mancinus; or the controversy over the child born from the second wife, while no divorce was issued to the first - in each of these, the most learned Jurists were sharply divided. Among such men, there was open and serious disagreement about what the Law itself was.

"And so, I ask you: What did Legal Knowledge offer the Orator in such Causes - when even the Jurists themselves did not agree? And when the man likely to prevail was not the one who mastered the Art proper to that Domain, but rather the one who possessed a different Art entirely - that is, not Civil-Knowledge, but Eloquence?

"I have often heard this story: When Publius Crassus was seeking the Aedileship, he was accompanied in his campaign by Servius Galba - older than him, already a Consular - because Crassus had pledged his daughter in marriage to Galba's son. It happened that a certain Rustic, seeking counsel, approached Crassus privately. After presenting his case, he received a response - technically correct, but clearly more attuned to legal formality than to the man's actual situation. When Galba saw the man departing, troubled and downcast, he called to him by name and inquired what matter he had brought to Crassus. Upon hearing it - and seeing the man's unease - Galba remarked, 'I see that Crassus has given you an answer while his mind was distracted and preoccupied.' Then Galba took Crassus by the hand and said: 'Come now - what could have possessed you to answer him so?'

"Crassus, a man deeply trained in the Law, replied with confidence that his judgment was correct, and that no doubt could exist in the matter. But Galba, shifting tone with subtle irony and rhetorical grace, began to offer analogies, drawing many comparisons, and speaking copiously in defense of Equity against strict

Law. And since Crassus could not match Galba in disputation - though he was counted among the Eloquent, he was in no way Galba's equal - he retreated to the support of authorities, citing passages from the writings of his brother Publius Mucius and from the commentaries of Sextus Aelius. And even then, Crassus finally conceded: Galba's argument seemed to him plausible - and nearly true.

LVII. Antonious: Presentation and Style

Antonious continued: "And yet - those Causes in which the point of Law admits no doubt at all are, generally speaking, never even brought to Judgment. Does anyone ever claim an inheritance under a Will made by a paterfamilias before the birth of his son? Of course not. Because it is universally understood that the birth of a son annuls the previous Will. In such clear matters of Law, therefore, there are no Trials. And so, the Orator may safely ignore this entire region of undisputed Law - which, without question, comprises the vast majority of all Civil Law.

"But as for those points of Law which even the most skilled Jurists debate? In such cases, it is never difficult for the Orator to find some Authority who supports the side he wishes to defend. And once the Orator has taken up those javelins - handed to him, as it were, already barbed - he hurls them not with the finesse of the Jurist, but with the full strength and sinew of his Orator's Arm.

"Unless, of course - if I may say this with all respect to that most excellent man, Scaevola - you, my friend, defended the Cause of Marcus Curius not with the arguments or teachings of your father-in-law, but with your own powers of Equity and your defense of Wills and the intention of the dead? Indeed, in my judgment - for I was often present, and heard you speak - you won over the greater part of that court not through Civil Knowledge, but through your Charm, and through the polished Wit of your delightful Irony. You mocked that overly sharp reasoning. You marveled, with theatrical admiration, at Scaevola's cleverness in asserting that a man must be born before he dies. You drew together a web of references - laws, Senate-decrees, and the customs of daily life and common speech - not only shrewdly, but also with humor and clever delight. And had we followed the words alone, rather than the substance, nothing could have been accomplished. The entire Trial, in fact, was full of joy and laughter - so much so that I do not see what benefit Civil Law brought to you there. But your power of Public-Speech - matched with extraordinary festivity and grace - was clearly decisive.

"As for Mucius himself - the guardian of his father's Law, the defender of his legal inheritance - what, in that Trial, did he produce that seemed drawn from the depths of Civil Law? What statute did he cite? What truth did he reveal that had previously been hidden from the untrained? No - his entire argument turned on this alone: that the written word must be obeyed above all. But even schoolboys rehearse such cases under their instructors - being trained in exercises where one side defends the Text, and the other appeals to Equity. And surely, in that Military Case you mentioned - if you had spoken either for the Heir or for the Soldier - you would not have resorted to the dry machinery of Hostilian formulas. No - you would have drawn upon your own strength, your Orator's Capacity. For if you had taken up the defense of a Will, you would have pleaded as though the entire Law of Wills itself were suspended upon that single Judgment. And if you had defended the Soldier's Cause, you - as you always do - would have summoned the Father from the grave by Speech alone. You would have made him stand before their eyes. He would have embraced his son - and, weeping, would have entrusted him to the Hundred Judges.

"By Hercules, you would have made even the stones weep and mourn. So that the entire phrase uti lingua nuncupassit - as he declared with his tongue - would not seem to come from the Twelve Tables (which you yourself prize above all the libraries of the world), but rather from the lips of a Master reciting verse.

LVIII. Antonious and Legal Knowledge

Antonious continued: "Now, as for your rebuke, Crassus - that the young display laziness for not mastering that Art, which you claim to be not only useful but exceedingly easy - I must ask: how easy can it be? Let those men answer who, relying on that very Art with supreme arrogance, go striding about as if it were the hardest thing in the world. And let you answer too - since you say that it is an Art so simple, and yet also concede that, strictly speaking, it is not an Art at all.

"Indeed, you admit it will only become an Art if someone first masters another, entirely different Art - so that this Legal Discipline might someday be completed through that. And yet, even as it stands incomplete, you expect it to be edified and adored. You argue also that it is full of delight. To this, I say: everyone willingly lets you enjoy such delight yourself. Let no one begrudge you that pleasure. But if someone were truly forced, right now, to learn something by rote - who among them would not rather Memorize Teucer from Pacuvius than commit to heart Manilian statutes on the sale of cattle and mules?

"And you invoke Love of Country - claiming we ought to know the discoveries of our Ancestors. But do you not see? Those ancient Laws have either grown moss-covered with age or have been repealed by newer statutes. You argue, further, that Good Men are made through Civil Law - because the Laws offer rewards to Virtue and penalties to Vice. But for my part, I always believed that Virtue - if it can be taught at all - must be cultivated through instruction and persuasion, not threats, violence, or fear. For even without any Legal Knowledge at all, we can surely recognize how noble it is to guard against evil.

"As for myself - since you, Crassus, grant to me alone the power to defend Causes without having learned Civil Law - I will say this in reply: I have never studied Civil Law. And yet, in those Causes where the matter turned upon the Law, I have never found myself wishing I had that Legal Knowledge. For there is a difference: to be the Artisan of some specialized Domain is one thing; to move about in Common Life and in the ordinary habits of men - not dull, not untrained - is quite another.

"Which of us, after all, is forbidden to visit our own farmlands? To look in on our vineyards and orchards - whether for gain or for simple pleasure? And yet, no one lives so blind or mindless a life as to not understand, at least in broad terms, what is planting and harvesting, or when and how pruning is done, or how vines are grafted. But if one must inspect a farm, or give instructions to a steward, or issue orders to a teamster - must he therefore study the agricultural manuals of Mago the Carthaginian? Or can he not simply rely on this shared human understanding?

"Why, then, should the same not be true in Civil Law - especially since we live our lives in the Forum, in negotiations, and in causes? Can we not be sufficiently prepared for such matters - at least so we are not Foreigners or Strangers in our own Republic? And if, now and then, a particularly difficult Cause is brought before us - what then? Is it so hard to confer with Scaevola here?

"And in fact, those whose Profession is Law - do they not already bring to us the very points most worthy of consideration, already examined and refined? Indeed - if the dispute concerns the thing itself, or the boundaries, or the property at issue (when we cannot examine it directly), or the documentation, or the phrasing of a contract - then we do not hesitate to learn the intricacies and complications. So if we must examine a Law, or consult an opinion of a learned man - why should we fear that, having not studied Civil Law in youth, we are somehow incapable of understanding it now?"

LIX. Antonious Rejects Roscius the Actor

Antonious continued: "So - does no benefit come to the Orator from knowledge of Civil Law? Certainly, I do not deny that any form of knowledge may be useful - especially to the Orator, whose wealth of Speech ought to be furnished with many resources. But I would insist that many things - both great and difficult - are already necessary for the Orator; and so, I would rather not see his energies dissipated into yet more disciplines.

"Take, for example: who would deny that, in the arrangement and movement of the Orator's body - the subtle positioning of hands, gaze, and stance - the grace and presence of Roscius the Actor could be of great use? Yet, I would advise no student of Oratory to labor over the gestures of the stage in the manner of professional actors.

"And what is more necessary to an Orator than the Voice? Still, on my recommendation, let no one train his voice in the manner of the Greek tragedians - those who spend years seated in practice, murmuring with closed eyes, slowly awakening the breath before each performance. They lie on their backs to warm the Voice, raising it in pitch, then dropping it again, until they sweep the full scale in a single breath - as if they were tuning a lyre, not preparing for Court. If we were to attempt such rehearsals - chanting paeans and hymns like temple-chanters - the clients whose causes we've agreed to argue would be condemned before we even opened our mouths in court!

"So then, if even in Gesture - which truly assists the Orator - and in Voice - which alone sustains and elevates Eloquence - we are not permitted to labor as much as we'd like, but must settle for what we can gain in the confines of daily civic toil, then how much less should we burden ourselves with the full discipline of Civil Law? That body of Law, after all, can be understood in outline without specialized training, and it is unlike gesture and voice in this key regard: Those Natural-Tools cannot be summoned on the spot from books or assistants. But the use of Law, in contrast, can be summoned suddenly - whether from a legal expert nearby, or a volume from one's library. In fact, those most eloquent of men often employ ministers of the Law when handling cases, even when they themselves are among the most learned. These assistants are what you, Crassus, just called pragmatici - legal practitioners who support the Orator's cause. And in this respect, our own Roman way is vastly superior: we have preferred, through the authority of our noblest citizens, to veil the laws and civil codes beneath a solemn dignity.

"Still, let it not be imagined that the Greeks overlooked this practice out of ignorance. If they had believed it necessary that the Orator be thoroughly trained in Civil Law himself, they would not have handed him a pragmatic helper - they would have made him learn the Law."

LX. Antonious: Leisure-with-Dignity

Antonious continued: "As for your remark, Crassus, that knowledge of Civil Law rescues Old-Age from loneliness - well then, so too, perhaps, does the possession of vast wealth. But our concern here is not with what may be useful to an old man - we are asking what is necessary for the Orator.

"And yet, since we've already drawn so many comparisons between the Orator and the Performer, let me continue: that same Roscius, whom we so often quote, is said to have claimed that as his age advanced, he would begin to prefer slower rhythms and softer melodies in his performances. Now if he - bound as he was by the strict measure and cadence of his Art - could still find such accommodations for Age, how much more easily may we, who are bound not to meter but to Matter, adjust our entire mode of speaking!

"And surely you, Crassus, are not unaware of how many styles of speaking exist - how various the forms of Oratory - and perhaps it was you yourself who first showed how powerful is a gentler and more measured style, such as the one you now frequently adopt. For even though you speak more calmly and mildly than you once did, this moderation of tone in no way diminishes the weight of your speech - indeed, it increases it. Many have excelled with this kind of speech: so we are told of Scipio and Laelius, who could settle even grave matters with speech barely more forceful than conversation. They did not - like Servius Galba - shout or strike their sides to be heard. So if even you - whether by choice or limitation - no longer choose to engage in such forceful speaking, are you truly afraid that your house, so noble in virtue and in citizenship, will be abandoned by the people merely because it is no longer besieged by legal clients?

"Far from it. Indeed, I hold the very opposite opinion: not only do I not believe that the crowd of litigants should be considered a bulwark of old age, I even long for that solitude you seem to dread - as if approaching a peaceful harbor. The greatest comfort for Old Age, in my judgment, is Leisure-with-Dignity. And as for the rest - that is, the value of History, of Public Law, of our Ancestral Path, and our treasure of Examples - if ever I should need them, I shall borrow from my dear friend, a man rich in such matters.

And I have no objection at all - indeed, I encourage - what you have just now advised: let our students read everything, listen to everything, and live fully within every field of upright study and human culture. But - by the gods! - I hardly think they will have enough time, if they intend to pursue all that you, Crassus, have laid down. For sudden exercises on proposed causes, thorough premeditated commentaries, that stylus of yours (which you rightly called the truest tutor and shaper of Speech) - these require no small labor. Even the practice of comparing one's own oration with the writings of others, or the spontaneous delivery of a response - be it praise, censure, confirmation, or refutation - based on someone else's text: all of this demands immense exertion, whether in Memory or in Imitation."

LXI. Antonious: Not Roscius, but Demosthenes

Antonious continued: "But that comparison, Crassus - that horrific image, as you called for each of us to become, in his own field, like a Roscius - I fear it may terrify more than it inspires. You claimed that it is not what is right that pleases, but that flaws, in their smallest form, cling to the audience's disdain more than any perfection earns applause. But I do not think this is true so much for us Orators as it is for actors.

"In the theater, I've seen Aesopus hissed for a mere slip in tone - where nothing is sought but pleasure of the ear. The moment pleasure dims, rejection follows. But in Oratory, many forces captivate: and even when not every part is perfect, the whole may yet be marvelous, simply because so much of it is great.

"Let us return, then, to that first definition: that an Orator is one who can speak with fitness for persuasion, as Crassus described. And let him be confined to those things in common use among citizens - in the ordinary courts and affairs of civic life. Let other disciplines, however grand or beautiful, be set aside; let him be pressed forward - night and day - in this one single task. Let him imitate Demosthenes, that Athenian to whom all agree the full force of eloquence was granted. We are told

Demosthenes had to conquer nature herself through labor. He stammered - unable to pronounce the first letter of the very Art to which he aspired! But through persistent training, he came to be thought the clearest speaker of all. When his breath was short and shallow, he practiced holding his voice through entire passages - his writings show that two full modulations of tone could be sustained without interruption.

"And more: it is said that, placing pebbles in his mouth, he trained himself to speak poetry aloud in full voice, without pause - on a single breath. Not standing still, but walking, climbing, pressing upward on steep slopes. These are the exhortations, Crassus, that I do indeed approve - by which young men may be stirred to labor and to study. But as for all the rest - that vast array of disciplines you gathered from every art and study - though you have indeed mastered them all, I must still hold that they lie outside the proper office and duty of the Orator."

LXII. The Day Concludes

When Antonius had spoken, Sulpicius and Cotta seemed, for a moment, to hesitate - unsure which of the two, in truth, had drawn nearer to the heart of the matter. Then Crassus, with a knowing smile said: "Antonius, you would have us believe the Orator is but a kind of laborer - an artisan of the Bench, pressed only by necessity and formed for utility. And I suspect - indeed I know - you do not wholly believe this yourself, but only wield that marvelous habit of refutation which no man has ever mastered better than you. That very skill - turning every argument to its opposite - is the exercise peculiarly proper to the Orator, though now it has been stolen away and domesticated among the Philosophers - especially those who, with great abundance, can argue both sides of every question.

"But I myself, especially before these listeners, did not think I was to describe only the kind of man who sits upon the bench and brings forth nothing more than necessity compels. I envisioned something greater - a figure who, in our Republic, should not be deprived of any form of adornment. You, however, since you have circumscribed the Orator's entire calling within such narrow boundaries, will now more easily explain the duties and precepts which we asked of you concerning the Orator's role. But I think" - he added, glancing at the sun - "we must leave that for tomorrow. We have spoken at great length already today.

"And now," he continued, "since Scaevola has resolved to go to Tusculum, he will rest awhile, until the heat of the day subsides - and we ourselves, at this hour, ought to give some attention to our health."

This pleased them all. Then Scaevola, rising, said: "Indeed," he said, "I rather wish I had not resolved to go to Tusculum today, Laelius. I would gladly have listened longer to Antonius."

And smiling, as he stood: "Nor was it so burdensome to me that our Civil Law was lightly shaken - as it was delightful to hear Antonius confess that he knew nothing of it at all."

www.ingramcontent.com/pod-product-compliance
Lightning Source LLC
Chambersburg PA
CBHW081647270326
41933CB00018B/3382